Group's Volunteer Leadership Series

JUMP START

Group

Loveland, Colorado

Group resources really work!

This Group resource incorporates our R.E.A.L. approach to ministry. It reinforces a growing friendship with Jesus, encourages long-term learning, and results in life transformation, because it's:

Relational—Learner-to-learner interaction enhances learning and builds Christian friendships.

Experiential—What learners experience through discussion and action sticks with them up to 9 times longer than what they simply hear or read.

Applicable—The aim of Christian education is to equip learners to be both hearers and doers of God's Word.

Learner-based—Learners understand and retain more when the learning process takes into consideration how they learn best.

Jump Start

Visit our website | group.com

Editor: Bob D'Ambrosio
Contributor: Marlene Wilson
Art Director: Amy Taylor

ISBN 978-0-7644-9769-8

Printed in the United States of America.

10 9 8 7 6 5 4 3 2 1 18 17 16 15 14 13

Contents

...Contents

Introduction

Imagine everyone involved in ministry!

Imagine walking into your church on a Sunday morning and seeing a beehive of activity…

- Classes hum along with energetic teachers ready to greet students.
- The music team is tuned up and ready to lead worship.
- The coffeepots are filled and percolating.
- Guests filter in through the doors because someone stopped by to visit newcomers in the community with fresh bread and invitations.

And it's all happening because at your church people are equipped and serving others. There's no scrambling around at the last minute—everything is right on schedule, right on time, right on target, and completely relaxed.

> "Imagine… everyone involved in ministry."

Imagine attending a church board meeting that's sharply focused, well-organized, and attended by people who can't think of anything else they'd rather be doing. People who are energized by the mission of the church and the purpose of the board.

And everyone around the table on that Thursday night is a volunteer.

Imagine walking down the hallway at church, glancing into offices where individuals and teams are busily pulling together the media for next week's worship service…providing counseling for a man who's in emotional pain…planning a youth group retreat…and rehearsing a drama that will introduce the message next weekend.

And everyone—in each room—is a volunteer.

Does it seem like a dream to have so many people so involved in important ministry? In some churches it is just a dream...but it doesn't need to stay a dream.

This book will help you turn your dreams of volunteer involvement into reality. There's nothing magical about the systems you'll discover. Many of the principles and procedures have been best practices with ministry leaders for decades.

Some are from the nonprofit sector, where they've worked equally well for just as long.

And some are from churches like yours that are a bit further along in the journey of creating a culture where volunteering is more than an obligation—it's a joy.

Maybe you're the pastor and you have a vision for a time when you're not the only one who's doing the work of ministry. You want to see volunteers join in the work of the church so you can have at least a little time with your family.

Maybe you're the christian education director or youth director and you'd like to see enough volunteers signed up to cover the small group or outreach ministry you'd love to start. You have a vision for what your area of ministry could be, and you're tired of settling for less.

Or maybe you're a board member or other volunteer who knows the fulfillment of being involved and used by God in ministry. You want to invite others who are now filling pews to be filling volunteer roles instead.

Imagine the power that would be realized if everyone offered to serve in an appropriate ministry role. How much could your church accomplish? What might you do that you simply can't do now?

> "See volunteers join in the work of the church."

Imagine how the members of your church would grow if they were actively, intentionally serving God and growing in their faith. If everyone came together on Sunday not for a quick spiritual pick-me-up but, instead, with exciting stories to share about how God is working through them.

Imagine how your church would grow if you had the reputation of being the place where people don't just talk about their faith, but work together to make things happen in your community. What if church members were constantly forming groups to enthusiastically meet real needs of real people? How packed would your new members class be? And how deep would you be growing in your faith?

If you have a vision for your church that includes any of the scenarios above, you need a fully functioning, healthy volunteer-equipping ministry. It won't be enough to keep improving your church's programs or to count on a remarkable pastor to draw new people to your worship services.

Excellent programs and a charismatic leader may help your church grow in attendance, but they won't help your church members grow deep in their faith or be satisfied with their spiritual growth. That takes involvement in ministry—which requires a volunteer culture that's working.

> You need a fully functioning, healthy volunteer equipping ministry.

In a *Leadership* journal article, Eric Swanson reported about a survey he gave his church to determine if there was a relationship between ministering to others and spiritual growth. Swanson asked the question, "To what extent has your ministry or service to others affected your spiritual growth?" and received a 92 percent "positive" response. When Swanson dug deeper and asked how service to others compared with other spiritual disciplines such as Bible study and prayer, 63 percent of respondents reported service to others was equally significant in their spiritual growth, and 24 percent of respondents said service to others was more significant than Bible study or prayer![1]

But how do you involve the membership of your church in significant service and ministry when many people don't express the slightest interest in getting involved? There are ways to encourage that change, and in this book we'll walk you through that process.

It starts with building a firm foundation on solid biblical thinking about serving and ministry. There are several theologies you must embrace concerning how God has designed people and the church if you expect to see serving grow in your congregation.

Later in this book you'll do a quick assessment of how "volunteer-friendly" your church culture is and identify obstacles that might be blocking your progress.

Finally, you'll craft a vision for where you want to be.

This book is all about understanding what you believe as a church, where you're starting your journey, and where you want to go. It may feel as if you're not diving quickly enough into shaping up your volunteer-equipping ministry, and you may be tempted to skip over this "vision stuff."

Don't.

It's your vision for where you want to go that sets the direction of your entire volunteer ministry. This is the foundation on which you'll build the culture. Skipping these key steps is like staking out a place to build a house on a beach and building your house on sand—and we all know how that turns out.

> "It's your vision...that sets the direction of your entire volunteer ministry."

Are you ready to launch or expand your volunteer-equipping ministry? Ready for changes that will dramatically increase the number of people in your church who are enthusiastically serving?

Wonderful! Let's begin...with you and what you believe about volunteers.

1. Eric Swanson, "What You Get from Giving" sidebar in " 'Great to Good' Churches," Leadership, Spring 2003, Vol. XXIV, No. 2, 38.

1 The Biblical Foundation for Serving

What do you believe about serving and ministry? Here's a quick look at three theologies that are the foundation for volunteer leadership in the church.

Don't you love the question *what if?*

When we ask *what if?*, we can begin picturing what tomorrow might be like. Asking that question invites us to cooperate with God in imagining a vision for the future.

Your church will have a future—next week, next year, and beyond. Wouldn't it be best if your church had the future you prefer? One that's grounded in God's will for your congregation, that's spiritually healthy, and that's moving forward to do God's will in your community?

When it comes to involving volunteers in your church, there's no secret about what God wants to accomplish. It's all there in the Bible, and it is reflected in three interrelated theologies. Let's explore these together. As we go, think about your church and how you're living out these three theologies.

The Priesthood of All Believers

True or false?—God intends for every member of your church to be active in ministry.

True! According to Scripture, we're all called to be active in the ministry of the church. God never intended for church to be a spectator sport. Just the opposite is what God has in mind, as we see in this passage:

> *But you are a chosen people, a royal priesthood, a holy nation, a people belonging to God, that you may declare*

the praises of him who called you out of darkness into his wonderful light. (1 Peter 2:9)

That "royal priesthood" is for all Christians, not just professional clergy. Men and women—we're all part of the priesthood of all believers.

Age doesn't have anything to do with it, either. In the same way we're not expected to retire from service when we get to the age of 65, neither are we too young to be involved when we're in sixth grade. When you think of who's been called by God to be involved in ministry, include your entire congregation.

> Is it evident that you believe everyone has a place in ministry?

When someone walks into your church, is it evident that you believe everyone has a place in ministry? Or is significant ministry done just by the paid staff or a handful of people? Maybe ministry is being done by just a few people because no one else will do it, but what's your preference? Does your church have an openness to lay people assuming ministry roles?

Because if that's God's expectation—that lay people will have ministry opportunity—we'd better be providing those opportunities. Failing to do so only cripples the church.

I think there's ample evidence in Scripture that God is looking for us all to roll up our sleeves and get involved. When we made a commitment to God, he made a claim on our lives.

Paul wrote:

Do you not know that your body is a temple of the Holy Spirit, who is in you, whom you have received from God? You are not your own; you were bought at a price. (1 Corinthians 6:19-20a)

In the book of Romans we read:

> *What then? Shall we sin because we are not under law but under grace? By no means! Don't you know that when you offer yourselves to someone to obey him as slaves, you are slaves to the one whom you obey—whether you are slaves to sin, which leads to death, or to obedience, which leads to righteousness? But thanks be to God that, though you used to be slaves to sin, you wholeheartedly obeyed the form of teaching to which you were entrusted.* (Romans 6:15-17)

Bought at a price.

Slaves.

Those words communicate that God owns us. He's paid for us. We're his. If he's got work to do, it's clear that we're all on his payroll. He wants to use us all.

Not everyone will preach, teach, or sing in the choir. But all Christians are supposed to be doing something that fits within their unique blend of abilities, skills, and passions. It's really not optional. Priesthood is all about *doing* something as well as *believing* something.

> "Priesthood is all about *doing* something as well as *believing* something."

What's the evidence in your church that you embrace the priesthood of all believers? Do church members see volunteers serving in significant and varied roles? Do they see every category of person involved in ministry of some sort?

If not, is your church willing to change?

By the way, here's the first place you should make changes: in the expectations of your leaders and lay membership.

When Jesus recruited his disciples, he called them to leave their businesses and families. It cost those fishermen something to follow Jesus. It often costs us little to follow Jesus, at least in the Western world. People expect to go to church and drop money in the offering plate, but that's about it.

So no wonder lay people look surprised when we explain they also need to serve in a ministry. It may be the first time they've heard they're required to do anything beyond showing up and writing a check.

We tell people all about the Savior Jesus. We teach about how Jesus saves people from their sins, loves them, and is preparing a place for them in heaven.

But we sometimes forget to mention much about the Lord Jesus.

The Lord Jesus calls everyone who follows him into the royal priesthood, where service and discipleship are more than theories—they're expectations. Joining a church isn't an invitation to retire; it's enlistment in an organization that's actively serving God. If you're going to expect people to serve in ministry, say so up front in your teaching and preaching.

- *Does* your church invite every member to be in appropriate ministry somehow?
- *Is* there a place for each person in your church to do ministry? Are you open to an influx of volunteers?

The Giftedness of Each Child of God

The Bible tells us that every believer can do ministry in some way. Each person has important work to do in the church, regardless of gender, age, or education.

Here's what Paul wrote:

> *For we are God's workmanship, created in Christ Jesus to do good works, which God prepared in advance for us to do.* (Ephesians 2:10)

And again he wrote:

> *And in the church God has appointed first of all apostles, second prophets, third teachers, then workers of miracles, also those having gifts of healing, those able to help others, those with gifts of administration, and those speaking in different kinds of tongues. Are all apostles? Are all prophets? Are all teachers? Do all work miracles? Do all have gifts of healing? Do all speak in tongues? Do all interpret? But eagerly desire the greater gifts. And now I will show you the most excellent way.* (1 Corinthians 12:28-31)

Finally, consider this passage in Romans:

> *If it is serving, let him serve; if it is teaching, let him teach; if it is encouraging, let him encourage; if it is contributing to the needs of others, let him give generously; if it is leadership, let him govern diligently; if it is showing mercy, let him do it cheerfully.* (Romans 12:7-8)

Clearly, believers' God-given abilities, skills, and passions are to be used to build up the body of Christ and to glorify God. Those are the truths wrapped up in the theology of "the giftedness of each child of God."

Our job is to help people discover where to put those abilities, skills, and passions to use. We need to do it for the health of the church and also for the spiritual health of individual believers.

Our job is to help people discover where to put those abilities, skills, and passions to use.

But before you embark on that journey, you need to decide:

- *Do* you believe each person in your church has something valuable to contribute?
- *Are* you willing to help people who aren't sure what they can offer to discover ways to serve?
- *Will* your church make room for people to serve in ways that align with their abilities, skills, and passions?

The Whole Body of Christ

In the same way each believer has a God-given ability, skill, or passion to use in ministry, each believer has a particular function in the body of Christ. We all fit *somewhere,* but we don't all fit *everywhere*. There's a big difference.

The theology of "the whole body of Christ" acknowledges that each member of your church has something to offer, but it's a specific something. People aren't interchangeable; you can't just move them around on the organizational chart. Someone God has designed to be an empathic, caring people-helper isn't going to thrive in a volunteer role that's designed to enter data on a spreadsheet. If someone's a hand, he or she won't fit a role designed for a foot.

The ministries in our churches are enhanced, changed, and expanded when we discover people's gifts and abilities. We get the right people in the right ministry, and everyone benefits.

Consider these passages...

> *It was he who gave some to be apostles, some to be prophets, some to be evangelists, and some to be pastors and teachers, to prepare God's people for works of service, so that the body of Christ may be built up until we all reach unity in the faith and in the knowledge of the Son of God and become mature, attaining to the whole measure of the fullness of Christ.* (Ephesians 4:11-13)

Now the body is not made up of one part but of many. If the foot should say, "Because I am not a hand, I do not belong to the body," it would not for that reason cease to be part of the body. And if the ear should say, "Because I am not an eye, I do not belong to the body," it would not for that reason cease to be part of the body. If the whole body were an eye, where would the sense of hearing be? If the whole body were an ear, where would the sense of smell be? But in fact God has arranged the parts in the body, every one of them, just as he wanted them to be. If they were all one part, where would the body be? As it is, there are many parts, but one body.

The eye cannot say to the hand, "I don't need you!" And the head cannot say to the feet, "I don't need you!" On the contrary, those parts of the body that seem to be weaker are indispensable, and the parts that we think are less honorable we treat with special honor. And the parts that are unpresentable are treated with special modesty, while our presentable parts need no special treatment. But God has combined the members of the body and has given greater honor to the parts that lacked it, so that there should be no division in the body, but that its parts should have equal concern for each other. If one part suffers, every part suffers with it; if one part is honored, every part rejoices with it. Now you are the body of Christ, and each one of you is a part of it." (1 Corinthians 12:14-27)

Are you willing to encourage people to minister within the constraints of their unique abilities, talents, and passions? If not, how do you expect those volunteers to be successful and fulfilled?

Are you willing to not do programs if you can't staff them appropriately?

Now let's ask a few *what-if* questions about your church—and mine.

What if we took seriously the implications of our theology when it comes to serving in our churches?

What if we reflected biblical principles in our policies and procedures when it comes to inviting and equipping volunteers in our churches?

What if we learned from our brothers and sisters in Christ who have found ways to connect serving to discipleship—and we put their experience to good use in our churches?

I'll tell you what will happen in most churches when *what if* becomes reality: We'll see dramatic and profound changes.

That's because in most churches, volunteerism is suffering. Most of the work of the church is done by the hired staff or a small group of volunteers. The vast majority of church members sit and watch, or, at best, are peripherally involved. They certainly don't find any meaning in their service through the church.

Wouldn't it be wonderful if serving in and through the church became the norm instead of the exception? What if the days when you had to beg for volunteers faded into a distant memory because people were actively seeking to serve? Wouldn't that be a welcome change?

The question is: How do we get from where we are to where we want to go?

> "Change does not happen overnight."

This book will help you, but it's a journey and a process. There's no pixie dust you can sprinkle on your church directory and find that, suddenly, calls will pour in from willing volunteers. Change does not happen overnight.

But the churches that grow successful volunteer equipping all have three things in common, and this is the place to briefly talk about them.

- **They approach the process prayerfully.**

  Sometimes the apathy in the pews toward doing the work of the church is a spiritual issue. It can't be fixed by doing a better job writing volunteer position descriptions. Nor can it be fixed by initiating a new process. It has to be fixed through what is called a "heart transplant," a renewing and refreshing of the heart.

  Your church might just need a change of heart about serving God and serving the church. And that gets fixed through prayer and through sharing God's vision for what your church could be as God's representative in your community.

  Will you commit to pray for your church? For your leaders, for your vision and mission, and for the members of your church who are willing volunteers—and those who aren't? They all need prayer.

- **They embrace the entire process.**

  This can't be stressed enough: *You must embrace the entire process we'll be describing.* If you pick and choose an idea here and a process there, you'll see improvement. It's all good stuff and it works. But you'll be sticking an adhesive bandage over a broken bone.

  You're already doing many things right. If you're like most people who are responsible for finding, recruiting, training, and maintaining volunteers, you have strong communication skills. You're already experiencing some success at the process just described.

  The problem is that the processes mentioned—finding, recruiting, training, and maintaining volunteers—are missing several key components. You may be excellent at all those things; you've still skipped important steps. Until you have them all, your effectiveness and results will be compromised. Your success will be limited, and you'll have to work harder.

  A process for placing volunteers in ministry that assures you—and the volunteers—that you'll have the right people in the right positions involves church-wide systems.

- **They build programs on a solid biblical foundation.**

  The three theologies we examined aren't new. We've all nodded in agreement as we've heard them preached and taught. But do we *believe* them? And if we *do* believe them, are the actions and attitudes expressed in our churches consistent with them?

  Those three theologies are fundamental to your church's volunteer culture. They reflect God's values when it comes to our doing kingdom work and how he has designed the church. When we let the values in these theologies slip, some terrible things can happen. Things that actually discourage serving.

  Consider this example of how a church leader chose to value a program over the people who were in his congregation...

The Little Drama Team That Couldn't

The pastor of a small church attended a conference hosted by a California megachurch. The pastor noticed how well drama was used in the megachurch's worship service, so he did a little investigating.

It turned out the drama ministry was comprised of a team of more than 50 people. They rehearsed regularly and performed two plays each year. They also sang musical numbers and performed skits each week that reinforced the sermon theme. They even had a sub-team of writers who did nothing but create original skits for the actors to perform.

The pastor couldn't wait to pull together a similar team back home. He just knew it would revolutionize his church's worship experiences.

So, two weeks after the pastor returned, he called a meeting for everyone interested in drama ministry. Two people showed up...and one was a junior high student who'd never been in a play.

The pastor made it a personal priority to get a team organized. He made another announcement and did a bit of personal recruiting. That got his team up to five. Still not enough.

So the pastor called a few of the perpetual volunteers—people who always said yes when asked directly—and twisted their arms. Reluctantly, two of those people joined, too, giving the team a total of seven members. Not ideal, but for a church of one hundred, not bad. Not bad at all.

It wasn't bad—it was worse than bad. The first skit was a disaster. Some of the team forgot lines. Others got stage fright and simply stood in place. The few people with an aptitude for drama couldn't pull the skit out of a tailspin. The effect was powerful—but not in the way the pastor wanted.

What went wrong? Plenty, but at heart it came down to this: *Most of the drama team was made up of people not gifted for this ministry.*

The pastor did respect the priesthood-of-all-believers theology—everyone was invited to participate in this ministry. But the pastor didn't respect the unique giftings of church members or their function in the body of Christ.

"Most of the drama team was made up of people not gifted for this ministry."

2 Navigating the Rapids of Change

Launching or improving the volunteer leadership process in your church forces change. Here's how to deal with it.

Initiating change in a church can be a difficult process. You may feel that now isn't the time to go through the pain of changing the way you interact with volunteers; you'll just make a few adjustments to your current volunteer process and hope that works.

As the experts suggest, that won't work. If you want to experience real change, you're going to have to do more than fiddle with a few loose wires. You've got to dig in and rebuild the engine. You've got to commit to making true changes, and it's going to take time.

The question for you: If not now, when will you make the changes? After you again experience a volunteer drought? After another batch of volunteers grows discouraged and quits? After yet another staff member moans about how nobody seems to care at your church?

> "It *is* tomorrow... We've got to act now to create the tomorrow we're envisioning."

Now is the time to start making changes. Today.

Have you heard the story of the kindergarten teacher? On the first day of school she asked, "Can anyone tell me what day it is?"

A bright-eyed little tyke raised her hand and declared, "It's tomorrow."

The kindergartner may not have had a firm grasp on the logistics of time, but she certainly understood the truth of time: It *is* tomorrow. Time is rushing by, and if we want things to be different in the future we've got to act now to create the tomorrow we're envisioning.

You may be feeling some urgency about changing how your church deals with volunteers. That's why you're reading this book. Honor that urgency—in most churches it's past time to initiate change. There's nothing to be gained by waiting longer to get started. Things won't get better by themselves, you know. Not without someone like you diving in and initiating change.

Tell me: If you had a friend who was experiencing a major health issue, would you suggest that she wait until things grew even worse before seeing a doctor? Of course not.

Would you suggest she live with the pain indefinitely because it might get better eventually? No—you'd urge her to get the help she needed right away.

Listen: If your church is experiencing pain in finding and keeping volunteers, it won't get better without intervention. You must act to initiate change, or you'll be stuck where you are today—forever. Is that what you want?

Here are two more *what-ifs* for your consideration:

What if we took God seriously enough to act on the theology we declare—even though it means dramatically changing how we do ministry?

What if we honored the urgency we feel to see change happen and we actually started initiating that change?

It boggles the mind what the church could become!

Consider the story of a church that has managed to implement the process we'll be sharing with you: Community Church of Joy in Glendale, Arizona. You may know them as a megachurch that has more than 10,000 members. That's who they are today, but when the church's pastor, Walt Kallestad, went to the church in 1978 there were just 200 members.

When Walt arrived, he and the church leadership discerned that they were uniquely called to missions, to reaching out to the unchurched. That's a mission and vision that energized some members but alienated others who wanted to maintain the status quo.

Once the vision was articulated, Walt saw some of the membership leave. It was a cost the church was willing to pay to get the entire church membership onto the same page and moving in the same direction.

To grow 50-fold in 25 years requires a church to stay open to change. What works when a church is at a membership of 400 won't necessarily work when membership reaches 4,000.

One change that came up on Pastor Kallestad's radar screen was a need for language to be friendly to unchurched people. Much of the traditional church jargon was a mystery to someone not raised in the church.

The woman who is in charge of the women's ministry was once one of those unchurched visitors. She kept coming back, even though at times she was uncertain what certain words meant. So she started keeping a list, and when the opportunity arose she asked Pastor Kallestad to define the terms. Words like "evangelism" and "atonement" held no meaning for her, but she suspected they must be important—they were always coming up in sermons.

After having to explain the meaning of church words a few times, Pastor Kallestad learned to change his language so he could connect with unchurched people. Because that was the stated mission of Community Church of Joy, learning a new way to communicate was worth the effort.

> Pastor Kallestad learned to change his language so he could connect with unchurched people.

Christian education courses were adapted so new members and visitors who had no Bible background at all could participate. When someone doesn't know if the book of Luke is in the Old Testament or New Testament, that changes how you approach teaching.

In time, it became apparent another change had to happen, too, and it concerned volunteers.

People with no church background—and there was an ever-increasing number of them involved in the congregation—were difficult to recruit as volunteers. They had no history of volunteering in the church. They had not grown up seeing their parents participate as volunteers. To these new members, attending a worship experience was like attending a play put on by a community theater: They were the audience. It never occurred to newly churched people that there was a role they could play in making things happen.

The congregation was already nearing 10,000 members, and church leadership expected they'd experience a new growth surge after the relocation to the new campus.

> "The work of ministry had to be passed to lay people... or there would be chaos."

Pastor Kallestad said, "We can't do it with our present structure." The work of ministry had to be passed to lay people more effectively than was happening or there would be chaos.

Keep in mind the church was growing. Good things were happening. Lots of churches hungry to experience the same sort of growth were visiting, taking notes. And the church already had lots of volunteers involved. The church leadership could have sat back and rested on its laurels.

But instead they felt an urgency to move ahead. To be even more effective. To be sure that the three theologies they supported with words were also supported in action.

Community Church of Joy followed these best practices...

- **They made a good thing better.**

  Remember, this was a church of more than 10,000 members. If you keep score by how many cars are in the parking lot, this church was already a clear winner. You'd think they'd just keep doing what they were already doing. It was working.

  Except they didn't keep score by counting cars. That number mattered to them, of course, but so did this number: How many people are involved in ministry? Getting people out of the pews and into service helped the church hang onto the new members it was attracting, and it also helped those people grow spiritually.

How are you keeping score at your church? If it's just cars, the impact you're having in your community is limited. If it's by how many people are involved in ministry, that's another issue altogether. Find out—it's a measurable number that's worth tracking.

- **They acted before they reached a crisis point.**

The growth the church expected after the move to a new campus materialized—so it's a good thing they revised their approach to working with volunteers first.

Was it convenient to change their volunteer-equipping approach while they were in the middle of planning a relocation? No—but it was important, because how volunteers were able to minister in and through the church was at least as significant a factor in meeting the needs of the unchurched as a new building.

- **They used sound management techniques to get organized.**

Do the words "management techniques" bother you? Sometimes in the church world we want to stay as far away from business practices as possible.

Call the process you use to work with people anything you want. "Management techniques" describes the process of organizing positions and people fairly well. But it doesn't matter what you call the process—so long as you do it. Community Church of Joy had some things organized—they didn't have people running around totally unsure what to do. But they couldn't tell how many volunteers they had or precisely what everyone was doing.

Like the Community Church of Joy, you must get organized or you'll have volunteers uncertain what to do because they don't have volunteer role descriptions. They won't know who they're reporting to or whether they've done a great job or a poor job. Projects will fail, people will be hurt, and the entire experience will be frustrating for everyone involved.

- **They adopted a process for volunteer leadership that will carry them into the future—no matter how large they grow.**

  You may be looking forward to seeing an attendance of 100. The idea of 10,000 people showing up is so far into the future you figure it will be your grandchildren who have to sort that out.

  But why not put the systems in place now that will encourage growth—and that will make sense when your church doubles or triples in size? It will only be more difficult to institute changes then.

  What's demanded of many congregations is this: change. Change is frightening in the best of circumstances. And when you're talking about changing church in some way—that's doubly frightening!

  But think about it this way: What will happen if you *don't* change how you manage the volunteer systems at your church? There are consequences either way, you know—if you act or if you fail to act.

  The unvarnished truth about change is this: It's difficult, often painful, and absolutely essential for the church to deal with if the church intends to remain healthy. Jesus never promised us insulation against change. God may be the same yesterday, today, and forever, but the church must be effective in communicating that unchanging love in quickly changing times. That takes flexibility and an ability to embrace change.

  > What will happen if you *don't* change how you manage the volunteer systems at your church?

  There have been times of stability throughout history, when the amount of change forced on people was minimal. That certainly doesn't describe life today! If life was a lazy, drifting river at one time, we're now hurtling down rapids and bouncing off rocks as we try to navigate quickly enough to stay afloat.

  We can learn a great deal about how to handle change from—quite literally—a whitewater rapids experience.

Eight Days, Seven Nights

Marlene Wilson shares the story of when she went on an eight-day raft trip down the Grand Canyon. That's the same canyon people point to as an example of how rushing water is so powerful it can slice through rock, slowly carving a chasm more than a mile deep and stretching as much as 18 miles from rim to rim. Any river that can do that sort of damage—even over an amazingly long time—is nothing to take lightly.

Normally, people consider the power of the Colorado River while staring down at it from a safe distance. From the rim of the canyon, the river looks almost picturesque. True, it's cascading down whitewater rapids, splashing a rainbow of spray high over boulders, but there's no danger... when you're standing on the rim.

But for eight days Marlene left the safety of the rim and rafted on that whitewater.

The questions she faced about leaving her comfort zone and climbing into a raft are the same questions you have to answer about initiating or improving your volunteer leadership process. Both situations call for handling fast and furious change. And both situations make for one hectic but exhilarating ride.

- **The first thing you need to do is address your motivation.**

  To some people, roughing it is staying at the Holiday Inn. They love the outdoors, but are not adventurers. Lying out under the stars by night and facing whitewater every day can be a stretch—a big stretch. So why go at all?

  For Marlene the answer was that it was going to be a once-in-a-lifetime experience, and she wanted to share it with her husband. She knew there would be whitewater involved and that it was going to stretch her beyond her comfort level to participate.

  When you're looking at initiating change in any organization—the church included—you can assume you're heading into whitewater. What's your motivation? Are you committed enough to see it all through?

- **Decide where you want to sit as you hit the rapids.**

  When rafting, you have to decide where to sit. It's not a casual question. When you sit at the front of a raft, you're the first one to make the acquaintance of any boulder you happen to hit, and you're the first person to dive down into the "holes" of swirling water that are everywhere on the river.

  If you're in the back of the raft, you'll find yourself lifted high when the raft dives into a hole. And if you're in the middle, you may feel safer, but don't be fooled—you'll be thrown around as the raft rocks and slams down the river.

  As you navigate change in your volunteer program, where are you sitting? Up front is where you get the most warning when something looms in front of you, and that seat gives you the best chance to respond.

  Don't back into change. Embrace it, and go for it.

- **Remember to take your sense of humor with you into the whitewater.**

  When you deal with change, it's essential you bring along your sense of humor. Without the ability to laugh, you're dead in the water. And if you get the chance, surround yourself with other people who know how to laugh, too.

  Find people who can laugh at life's challenges when you're heading for whitewater, and bring them along. You'll need the humor of friends when you hit the whitewater of change.

- **Prepare to experience some pain.**

  With change comes discomfort—and sometimes outright growing pains. But when you step outside your comfort zone, things happen.

  For Marlene, the pain started on the third day of her rafting trip. She broke her shoulder. It wasn't an obvious break; they later discovered she had two hairline fractures.

The fourth day of the trip was the last day a helicopter could come in and take Marlene out. If she wanted to get to a hospital, she had to decide to go immediately. If she went further downriver, she was making the entire trip—no matter what.

She decided to stay.

It wasn't a foolhardy decision; it was a decision that the pain she was experiencing was going to be part of the experience. She could handle it—but *was* forced to make some adjustments.

The process of energizing volunteer involvement won't go exactly as you've planned, no matter how well you do your planning. Something—or *several* somethings—will happen to impact you. You'll need to learn new skills. You'll need to adapt. And you'll be stronger for the effort.

Stay flexible and versatile. Remember there's seldom one right way to do something. You'll have to adapt. If you try something and it doesn't work, try something else. Don't get stuck. Don't become negative or obsessed with what fails. Move on.

Never settle for saying "People are too busy to volunteer." Instead, ask, "How could people volunteer if we structured things differently?"

- **Decide what you'll focus on—and what you'll let go.**

When big organizational change happens, we find a lot of people focus on the "ain't-it-awfuls?" and the "if-onlys," and people get stuck there. They can't let go of what once was or the comfort they once enjoyed.

One of the challenges of living in a changing, whitewater world is remaining an "optimistic pragmatist." By that we mean someone who sees the world realistically. We know there are difficulties that come with experiencing change. We know there are obstacles in the water in front. Choose to remain optimistic as you face those things, confident in a God who's going to be there with you through all of it, come what may.

You get to choose what to focus on, you know. Maybe half of your volunteers deserted the ship when you instituted accountability. Well, what about the half who stayed and flourished and the new people who were attracted to the volunteer program because it is well-organized now? Focus there.

You could think about the snide comments that came when you changed a process, or you could let those words go, forgiven by choice.

- **Realize not everyone can tolerate the same amount of change—or risk.**

  Change involves a certain amount of risk. Maybe nobody will *drown* if the music leader slips an old hymn in among the praise choruses your church has been using for the past few years, but there may be some negative comments. There's risk.

  If you're going to initiate change, you need to find people who are willing to go out on the edge with you. Build teams involving those people.

Only the very best guides lead trips down the Grand Canyon, and most guides frequently get out of their boat, climb up cliffs, and scan the river for several minutes before they return through the rapids.

Taking time to read the river is as important for sunburned old professional guides as it is for first-time rookies.

Guides know there are some principles that *don't* change: how water moves around rocks, what happens when oars are applied to the left side of the raft, how the boat moves through rapids. Those are the same—but the order in which they present themselves can change in the blink of an eye. And there can always be the first time something happens: a huge branch falls in just as the raft passes a cottonwood tree, or the seam on the raft splits.

When you enter the whitewater, change happens...sometimes at an alarming rate.

But we serve a God who is changeless in his love for us, and as we seek to involve his children in ministry we're cooperating with his purposes. The three theologies we've discussed are a firm foundation for instituting the process we're outlining. You stand on solid theological ground as change swirls around you.

May we suggest that part of your leadership role is to climb up on the high, sturdy cliff of God's love and read the river for your people. You'll be guiding them through the rapids of change, and you want to bring them into places of service and joy safely.

3 The Need for Visionary Leadership

Why one person—like you—can make a huge difference.

What will be required of you to put in place a process for volunteer equipping that respects the three theologies we've already discussed? *And* that makes use of the techniques we've learned through years of experience?

Prayer, certainly—because initiating change always needs prayer.

It will take time, too. Don't expect everyone to immediately see the wisdom in the changes you're making. You may well encounter resistance from some of the volunteers and staff.

Plan on effort being required. If you don't yet have descriptions of volunteer roles, they'll have to be written. If you don't have a top-notch training and orientation program, it needs to be created. This isn't an easy process, but the results you'll get will make any effort you invest worthwhile.

> "A leader is someone who dreams dreams and has visions, and can communicate those to others in such a way that they of their own free will say 'yes!'"
>
> Mike Murray

And you'll also need visionary leadership.

After all the reading, writing, and pondering about leadership that exists, a simple definition may be best described by Mike Murray, a Presbyterian pastor.

Mike says, "A leader is someone who dreams dreams and has visions and can communicate those to others in such a way that they of their own free will say 'yes!'"

Here's why this is a great definition. Having dreams and visions is not about where you are, but where you want to be.

Visionary leadership focuses less on the difficulties of today and more on where we'd be if we somehow got past our difficulties. It's a visionary way of seeing our situations. It's also a faithful way of seeing things.

It sounds easy, doesn't it? So why don't we do more of it in the church?

It may be because we're too busy doing, surviving, and coping to spend time thinking about the future and where we're heading. When you've got a Sunday school to staff or a sermon to prepare, who has time to dream dreams—even at 10:00 p.m.?

One of our biggest challenges is to shift our basic paradigms about how we *do* leadership—not how we talk about it. And that takes vision.

One test of a good leader, rather than *How much have I done?* needs instead to be *How many others have I involved?* This entails *not* doing all the work but seeing that it's done and done well. This is an enormous shift for church leaders, but a shift that's absolutely crucial! To do it well requires the skills of sound volunteer leadership.

Here are a few more *what-ifs* you might want to ask:

> One test of a good leader needs to be *How many others have I involved?*

What if your pastor's job description changed so the pastor was rewarded for involving others rather than simply getting things done?

What if you asked people to recommend ministry initiatives based on the abilities, skills, and passions they could bring to the table?

What if every leader in your church received training about how to delegate well?

Group Publishing did a survey of pastors and discovered that very few had received formal training in working with volunteers...or in skills needed to work effectively with volunteers, like delegation.

That's right: It's possible to receive a post-graduate degree in ministry that does not include even one course in effectively working with volunteers, this in spite of the fact that pastors will spend their entire careers working in volunteer-based organizations.

If we're serious about volunteer ministries thriving, let's prepare our leadership to value and embrace them.

And then there's the rest of Mike Murray's definition of leadership: the ability to "communicate those [dreams and visions] to others in such a way that they of their own free will say 'yes!'"

This wonderfully sums up the respect leaders need to have for volunteers.

There's no room for coercion when recruiting volunteers. There's no room for manipulation. There's always room for presenting a vision, dream, or mission and letting volunteers who are drawn to it respond with an enthusiastic "yes" that will drive their dedicated service.

The clearer the vision and the more enthusiastically committed to the vision the leaders are, the more likely it is people will catch the vision.

The clearer the vision and the more enthusiastically committed to the vision the leaders are, the more likely it is people will catch the vision. Volunteers have to see, feel, and experience the excitement and clearly understand how they can help make the dream or vision happen.

When it comes to providing leadership in a volunteer setting, skills of strategy and advocacy are much more important than mere oratory. There are few places where talk is cheaper or action more necessary.

Here's a story that illustrates Mike's definition of leadership in action.

Mikey Weiss and 200 Flats of Raspberries

Mikey Weiss retired in 1987 after 40 years in the Los Angeles produce business. One day, Mikey visited his son's produce firm at the L.A. wholesale market just in time to see a forklift hoist 200 flats of raspberries into a dumpster. The fruit was unmarketable, but still edible.

Mikey, watching, had an "aha" moment, and a *what-if* question occurred to him.

Six hundred people were going hungry in a tent city just five miles away. Mikey thought, *What if I could find a way to get produce wholesalers to stop dumping their surplus and instead donate it to organizations that feed the hungry?* That was the day the Los Angeles Charitable Food Distribution Project was born.

Mikey pitched his idea to his produce colleagues, who caught his vision and agreed to help. An extensive volunteer network formed to collect and distribute produce from wholesalers in the area. After hearing about Mikey's efforts, two University of Southern California professors took Mikey's vision even further. They created a model framework of the L.A. project with the goal of helping other cities create similar programs. After all, if it was a good idea in L.A., why wouldn't it be a good idea in Detroit or Des Moines?

Their organization, From the Wholesaler to the Hungry (FWH), has advised and assisted over 38 communities across the country in developing perishable food recovery programs.

One person. One *what-if* moment. One vision. And because of a vision that was communicated clearly and in a way that others could choose to enthusiastically embrace with a "yes," thousands of people were fed.

What are your *what-ifs*?

In these turbulent times, you can't afford for your church's mission to be fuzzy or out of focus. If you want to inspire volunteers to get behind programs and projects, you'll need to share your vision in a clear, compelling fashion. And you've got to make room in that vision for the participation and ownership of church members.

Hang onto that insight: You must make room in your vision for the participation and ownership of church members.

We have a picture of visionary leadership being like Moses coming down the mountainside, carrying tablets etched with the Word of God. Moses wasn't coming to negotiate or to invite commentary. He was there to announce that there was a new law, a new relationship with God. He was proclaiming a vision, and it was up to everyone to get behind it. Period.

> You must make room in your vision for the participation and ownership of church members.

But your vision of adding a second service probably doesn't come with that sort of clear-cut, God-given authority. If you want to enlist help making the vision come to pass, you're going to have to be more flexible than Moses was.

The nuts and bolts of turning a vision into a reality reside in the people who carefully craft, plan, and nurture the vision. People like you. People like your church leadership. People like your church membership. This is why volunteer leadership is important—absolutely *vital*—in the world and in the church.

Outstanding, ongoing volunteer participation doesn't just happen; it requires careful nurturing and direction. And it's worth the effort to build excellent volunteer participation.

Why? For many reasons...

- **Active participation in ministry often blocks the revolving door that's part of many churches.**

  In many congregations there are two key numbers that should be measured—but we keep track of just one of them.

The first number represents the number of people who have started attending the church in the past month. The second number represents the number of people who have *quit* attending the church in the past month.

We measure the first number but often have no accurate idea about the second number. And while we know that people leave and go elsewhere, we don't really know why. There's no reliable mechanism in place to do "exit interviews" to reveal why people chose to leave. They simply disappeared through the revolving door that lets people in and lets people out.

Do this: See what impact getting involved in a ministry position has on the commitment—and longevity—of your membership. Check the numbers. We're willing to bet that the group of people who have been plugged into appropriate volunteer roles and who are finding meaning in those service opportunities are far likelier to stay—and flourish.

- **The world needs what the church offers and the good news we proclaim.**

These are days that can be discouraging, because even though we know that in the end good will prevail, it certainly doesn't *feel* that way. Not when we see the crime statistics or drive through burned-out, boarded-up neighborhoods.

We can be despairing, believing things will never get better. Or we can be motivated to reach out, asking God to use us in some small way. Christ-followers choose to reach out. They choose hope.

And the world needs all the reaching out and hope it can get.

Our friend in ministry Nancy Gaston told us about a woman who phoned her about participating as a volunteer in her church.

> *Eileen phoned the Lay Ministry Director with a request. She was recovering from a bout of severe depression and anxiety and was hoping to re-enter the workforce. However, she wasn't sure she had the focus and stamina to work a full day. Was there a job she could do on her own schedule, gradually increasing the daily hours?*

There was. We assigned her the task of cleaning and reorganizing the supply room for the church school program. Coming in daily, she planned the work herself, checking occasionally to make sure her system was acceptable.

At first she came and went without saying much, but as the daily hours increased, she shared coffee breaks and lunchtime with staff and volunteers—interacting with increasing ease. By the third week, she was working full days and soon completed the task. The supply room looked wonderful, transformed from disorderly piles to organized and brightly labeled shelves.

We wrote her a letter of thanks and commendation to share with prospective employers, and Eileen started attending worship at the invitation of a volunteer she met over coffee. A month later, she called to say she had a full-time job as a warehouse manager.

Eileen told us, "I never knew I could organize things like that until you gave me a chance to try it. I feel like a new person—a competent one."

Eileen needed what the church had to offer, and the way she plugged in and got involved was through serving. Imagine the impact that church would have if it was intentional about including outside volunteers in community-based projects like cleaning a park or planting flowers along a public walkway.

We must build relational bridges if we intend to carry the gospel to people.

We must build relational bridges if we intend to carry the gospel to people. Serving is an excellent way to bring people together.

- **As we capably manage volunteerism, we create opportunities for people to be at their best as they help others.**

  A corporate human resource director once said to his pastor, "You're so lucky to be working with volunteers. You get to be with people when they're at their best."

  He was right. People *are* at their best when they're so committed to a mission that they set aside their own agendas. When you're stacking sandbags next to a swollen river, standing ankle deep in mud and soaked from a cold, stinging rain, you've got lots of reasons to complain. You're wet and tired. The work is backbreaking. There's no hot coffee. But you and three dozen other Red Cross Disaster Team volunteers are saving a neighborhood, so nobody cares. Moments like that are when people are at their very best in service to others.

  Those moments change the lives of people helped, but they change the lives of volunteers, too.

  Consider what Stephanie Adams had to say about a volunteer project in which she became involved…

  > *Our church was doing a number of community outreach projects during the Christmas season. This particular project was at the Women in Crisis shelter. Our group went in to do some painting and cleaning of the shelter. So the job itself wasn't that special: paint and wallpaper a bathroom. In everyday life that's no big deal.*
  >
  > *What affected me was being in the shelter, a place of refuge for so many women who leave home with no possessions, no belongings, often just the clothes on their back. I glanced into rooms that mothers shared with their babies and children. These were women looking for safety and a new start.*
  >
  > *After we'd finished for the day, I was relaxing at home when the full impact hit me. There I sat, in my beautiful home, the Christmas tree lit, safe and secure in the knowledge that I was warm and surrounded by love. Blessing and sadness both overwhelmed me.*

Blessing, because I knew that God loved me and that everything that I have (and not just the material stuff) comes from him. Yet, at the same time, incredible sadness, because for a part of a day, I was in a place where warmth, love, and security didn't exist for many residents.

Volunteering has never been the same since. Now, whatever I do, it's a grateful response for all the blessings that God has bestowed on me.

- **It creates new meaning and purpose in people's lives when they discover and use their God-given talents and abilities to make a difference.**

  A newly divorced woman once walked into the Volunteer Center in Boulder, Colorado. She was new to the area, new to a life without her husband, and she wanted to volunteer at the center. Her realtor had suggested she get to know people by working at the center.

  The woman indicated she'd had a career as a secretary before getting married 25 years earlier. She said she'd enjoyed it, and the center needed a volunteer secretary, so they put her to work.

  By the end of her first day, it was clear 25 years away from typing had taken their toll. Every letter she'd typed was filled with errors.

  But here's what happened: She took a typing course and sharpened up those skills. Within a few years she became the supervisor for all the office volunteers. A few years later she was taking on even more responsibility.

  Seven years after she walked into the Volunteer Center, she left—to become the paid director of the Big Sisters program in Boulder. Her time with the Center turned out to be a seven-year internship that prepared her for a new profession at which she excelled.

- **Involvement in meaningful volunteer efforts can create hope for those who are experiencing life's difficulties.**

  Lynn, a volunteer in the Big Brother program, says, "It was a life-changing experience for me, but it had an amazing impact on Brian, my little brother. I couldn't believe what one morning per week did in his life. He and his mom met with social workers all the time, but nothing changed until a guy showed up to take him out for a pizza."

  Of course. Think about it from Brian's perspective for a moment. This volunteer set aside Saturdays to spend time with Brian *by choice*. It wasn't the volunteer's job to take Brian fishing or to talk about school as they kicked through a field looking for arrowheads. No wonder Brian felt special and listened carefully when the volunteer talked.

  > Something amazing happens when we receive time or services from volunteers: We feel worthy.

  Something amazing happens when we receive time or services from volunteers: We feel worthy. We know it's not part of that person's job to help us. It's a gift, and that makes a Saturday morning of time so much more precious. It's not *just* time—it's hope that things will get better.

  Nancy Gaston has encountered how God has used volunteer positions to dramatically help the volunteers as well as the people the volunteer is serving.

  When Nancy's church distributed a talents and interests survey, one person who responded was a woman named Kelli. Here's what Nancy says about what happened.

  > *None of us on the Lay Ministry Team knew Kelli—she was a member who seldom attended, wasn't involved, and didn't seem to socialize with other members. Kelli had marked "office support" on her questionnaire—the only item she expressed any interest in.*
  >
  > *So the office administrator invited Kelli to come for an interview. She came but was so shy and withdrawn she didn't even make eye contact. A woman of about 70, Kelli was*

a recent widow who apparently seldom left her house. She agreed to come in for half a day per week to do copying and collating.

Gradually, Kelli warmed to the work as well as to the other volunteers and staff. She started to bring snacks to share and started to show her sly sense of humor. After about six months, she was the person organizing groups to do mailings. She instructed the other volunteers assertively and looked them in the eye. And after a year or so, she began "seeing" a neighbor who was a widower. They began to attend church together and even stayed for fellowship time—something Kelli had never done before.

And her "gentleman friend" comes along to help in the office on occasion.

- **When we work together, we create moments and pockets of real community and collaboration.**

  Visit a Habitat for Humanity worksite and you'll see something you don't often find in the world: a place where titles, roles, gender, color, and age don't matter. Not when everyone is working together for a mission everyone believes in.

  You'll often find CEOs swinging hammers alongside teenagers. And when a piece of lumber is hauled past, there may be a successful businessman carrying one end and an economically-challenged single mother carrying the other end. Where else would such a diverse group of people come together to accomplish a task?

  Volunteer opportunities can bring together people who would never get to know each other in any other way. Even in the church, we tend to cluster with our own friends, people who are like us and with whom we have a shared history. Community doesn't automatically happen just because we park in the same parking lot and sit through the same worship service.

But when there's a *what-if* that binds us together, barriers go down. Relationships form. Tasks are shared. Community is experienced.

What you do to encourage serving is important, so it's worth doing well. It's more than simply organizing schedules—it's ministry to those who volunteer, to those whom the volunteers serve, and to the God who pours out talents, abilities, and passions to be used for him.

Let's not settle for "good enough" when it comes to volunteer leadership.

Let's give it our best.

Determining If Your Church Culture Is Volunteer-Friendly

Take the temperature of your church to determine if it's volunteer-friendly or volunteer-toxic. Here's a test—and ideas for fixing what's broken. Also—the Core Values of Volunteer Leadership!

We don't want to assume that we know exactly where you are as you begin your journey toward launching or improving your volunteer-equipping process. Maybe you have a good system in place and it's pretty much easy pedaling for you to get where you need to go.

But maybe it's an uphill climb to get even one person to volunteer for a role at church. You're huffing and puffing and barely making any headway at all. *Anything* would be an improvement over what you're experiencing at your church.

Each of you has your own unique situation, size, history, perspective, and role in the church. Some of you have a long experience working with volunteers, and some of you are new to the field. Some of you are confident, and some of you question God's wisdom in putting you anywhere near the responsibility of helping volunteers find the right fit as they seek to serve in the church.

But one thing you all have in common: *You are the experts where you are.* As we share tools and techniques with you, be open and flexible as you apply them. They must fit the reality of your unique situation to be useful.

For example, if you're a pastor or church leader who's looking for a system to revitalize your whole church's volunteer involvement and you need a centralized function to do it, you'll use the material one way. But if you're the director of children's ministry, youth director, music minister, or you're concerned primarily with finding volunteers for just one program in your church, you'll use this material differently.

> Grow toward centralizing the function of volunteer recruiment.

Both are legitimate uses of the volunteer insights and process you'll learn. But I would encourage you to *grow toward centralizing the function of volunteer recruitment.* That's where you'll find the most benefit from putting these tools to use, as Community Church of Joy discovered.

A "director of equipping ministry" or "volunteer coordinator" may be the *last* position you can imagine being funded by your church. That position is just now beginning to emerge as a staff function in churches, and it's appearing—this is no surprise—first in churches with a large budget and large staff. But it *is* appearing, and we can foresee a day when the minister of volunteer involvement is as typical a staff position as children's ministry director is today.

Don't believe us? Wait until you see what putting in place a solid, sound process does for volunteer involvement for your church. In a year see how plugging people into service opportunities builds their commitment and retains them. Do a quick analysis of how many things you once paid to have done are being accomplished by volunteers. As ministry area leaders learn to delegate, see how they are more vibrant—and less burned out.

But no matter how you intend to use this material, it's probable you'll run into some obstacles. By discussing them now—before you collide with them—you'll be better prepared to overcome them. It's like pausing to read the river.

It probably won't be terribly helpful to hear this, but you may encounter resistance to launching or expanding volunteer involvement that has nothing to do with you. It's not personal. It's cultural.

There are attitudes and behaviors regarding volunteers that are toxic to a healthy church, and they may have taken root in your church culture decades ago. Place a check in the box next to any you've seen or experienced in your church.

Toxic Attitudes and Behaviors

☐ **Team leaders end up doing all the work on their teams.**

This can happen for a number of reasons. It may be that no one ever signed up to serve on the team, so a single zealot took the project and ran with it. That happens, though it's seldom the best approach.

Another thing that happens is equally bad, if not worse. There *is* a team, and it may even be comprised of volunteers who want to serve. But because the team leader won't define what needs to be done or isn't willing or able to share power through delegation, it turns into a one-person show.

For example, suppose Jenny Smith is the newly elected leader of the Christian education department. She has a new group of team members sitting around the table in the church hall. It's their first meeting.

Jenny introduces herself and talks about why the project is important, provides information about what's been done in the past, and describes her vision for the future. She covers a remarkable amount of material, hands out printouts, and then closes with prayer.

It's not until the meeting is over that most of the team members realize that the only person who did any talking was Jenny.

The second meeting comes up on the calendar, and once more the team sits around a table. And once more they hear Jenny tell everyone what she's accomplished. And once again the members of the team go home without really needing to be at the meeting. They contributed nothing. They were asked to do nothing.

There's no third meeting.

If you have people in places of leadership who don't know how to delegate, are you willing to provide training?

☐ **A handful of people (the Pillars) do all the work, while the majority of people (the Pewsitters) watch.**

Here's what often happens in churches...

The Pillars are those folks who show up for church each week and who also can be counted on when it's time for the fall festival, the spring father-daughter dance, and the living nativity. They even take a week off work so they can help at vacation Bible school.

Because they *are* so involved, the Pillars have become buddies. And because they're buddies, they usually call each other when it's time to recruit for the next church program. Alisa calls Tricia and says, "Remember when I helped you out on mission weekend? Well, I need your help at the silent auction." They end up creating a club of sorts, one that isn't always open to new members.

> "Are your leaders burned out? Place a time limit on volunteer roles."

Plus, the motivation to participate is often tinged with guilt. Tricia can't very well say no after Alisa housed two missionaries and also made authentic Russian food for the missionary banquet.

It may be that your church's Pillars aren't inclusive of new volunteers. Before you assume that Pewsitters refuse to get involved, find out how effectively Pewsitters are being invited to serve.

And also find out if the Pillars are making all the decisions about church projects and programs. If that's the case, it's no wonder the Pewsitters aren't excited about getting involved. They have no ownership.

- [ ] **Leaders are asked to cover several major jobs at once—and them far too long.**

There are churches that refuse to let someone be in charge of more than one ministry area. Why? Because each ministry area is worthy of having someone focus his or her best energies on it and because when you stretch people too thin, they tend to snap.

Are your leaders burned out? Have they passed the point where their passion sizzles into plain obligation? That didn't happen by accident, and the cause is often overcommitment.

One quick way to be assured you won't have this problem continue is to place a time limit on volunteer roles. Set a reasonable term for service, and make it part of the volunteer ministry description. That way people know how long they're expected to serve and how to pace themselves. Volunteers can leave the role when their term of service is over, or—if you're both in agreement—they can sign up for another term of service.

Some churches also set a limit on how many terms someone can serve in the same volunteer role. If you have a wonderful small group leader who's serving in an area of talent, skill, and passion, it may make little sense to remove that person simply because some calendar pages have flipped over. But if you have someone who's staked out the nursery as her private kingdom and refuses to make changes or to include others, you'll be glad you have a policy about terms of service.

- [ ] **Leaders require unrealistic time commitments that scare volunteers away.**

Accepting a volunteer role shouldn't be a life sentence. When we ask potential volunteers to take on open-ended responsibilities ("You'll only be in charge until we find someone else"), we're doing a poor job of caring for our volunteers. They know what will happen when they say yes: We'll quit looking for a replacement. We've got them, so why should we continue searching?

> "A volunteer role shouldn't be a life sentence."

There was a time that some volunteers practically lived at the church. These Pillars were the people who thrived on volunteering. But look around: You don't see many of those people around any longer. We can't create volunteer positions that are essentially part-time jobs. There must be "entry level" volunteer roles that are episodic or that require few hours.

Review your volunteer position descriptions: Are they so demanding that in a world of two-income families no one can fulfill them? Is either the duration or intensity of volunteer roles unreasonable?

Keep in mind that "unrealistic" is in the eye of the beholder when it comes to time commitments. A major trend in volunteerism is that volunteers prefer three-, six-, or one-month assignments rather than longer commitments. The shorter time commitments fit better into volunteers' busy lives.

☐ **There's no system for coaching volunteers.**

> What draws your volunteers to serve?

How long would you like to stay in a role where you're not sure you're doing well and there's no feedback? Or if a problem arises you don't know who to call for help? Not long. Yet that's what we do to many volunteers.

Is there a documented process by which you do evaluations of volunteers? If not, you're robbing them of the opportunity to get better in what they do. And that robs the people being served by your volunteers of the chance to be served by ever more excellent volunteers.

Plus, there's this: When your wonderful children's pastor leaves, will the program disappear with that person? If the pastor isn't developing a second line of leadership, everything ends when the pastor retires, goes to another church, or dies.

Some advice: If you have a program that's working well, *insist* that the leader of that program train others in the nuts and bolts of pulling the program off. You don't want to discover that nothing was ever written down the day after the founder of the program leaves.

☐ **Volunteers are more committed to a leader than to the mission.**

Especially if you have a very engaging, inspirational leader, you can have a situation arise in which if the leader leaves, the volunteers leave, too. The volunteers aren't committed to the mission and vision of the church; they're committed to "Pastor Tom."

What draws your volunteers to serve? A relationship with your church's leadership is good—but is it all there is? What is the relationship of your volunteers to the mission of the church?

☐ **Clergy and other leaders fail to delegate to volunteers because "It's quicker to do it myself," "I don't want to bother anyone," or "No one does it quite like I do it."**

What's insidious about this obstacle is that probably the staff member who dismisses volunteers as time-consuming is right: It *does* take time to direct volunteers. It *does* take time to bring someone up to speed on a task. It probably *is* quicker to do it yourself—if you want to do it yourself forever.

It's a variation on the old "Give a man a fish and you've fed him for a day; teach him to fish and he'll have food forever" proverb. A volunteer-centered version of that truism might be, "Teach a volunteer to prepare the bulletin inserts and it will take you four hours today. But next week you've got that four hours to go do something else."

Leading volunteers is an investment that will pay dividends—but not immediately. Are your staff and leaders willing to invest in volunteers?

> "Leading volunteers is an investment that will pay dividends—but not immediately."

Does your staff truly believe that volunteers *want* to be involved? that it's not a bother to volunteers to use their skills, talents, abilities, and passions in ministry? that it's fulfilling?

And is your staff willing to let loose of *how* a task might be accomplished, so long as it's done on time and meets the goal? Frank may *not* design the newsletter quite the same way you would...but does it matter? Can you give him a bit of room for creativity and ownership, as long as it's clear, accurate, and on time?

Any of these attitudes or behaviors can block your best efforts to involve more congregation members in volunteer ministry roles. Did you place a check in any of the boxes? If so, you've identified a toxic attitude or behavior you'll need to address.

And hear this: The more boxes you checked, the likelier your church is experiencing a lack of involvement by members and a decreasing membership. And why shouldn't people be drifting away? They're not church "members" in the full sense; they're church "attenders."

We've seen churches that actually *discourage* serving in the congregation. Pastors in those churches would object to that assessment, but it's true. The policies and procedures in place were so toxic to a good volunteer experience that there's no way the majority of church members could participate in a meaningful way.

> We've seen churches that actually *discourage* serving in the congregation.

Every volunteer-toxic attitude or behavior is an obstacle standing between you and where you want to go. If you intend to reach a place where you have a volunteer-friendly church culture, you'll have to go over, under, or around those obstacles—and that takes time and energy you don't have to spare. Plus, getting around them won't solve your problem. What's required is to *remove* those obstacles so the way is clear.

Before tackling the most common obstacles you're likely to face, we'd like to describe the attitudes and actions that typify a *healthy* church volunteer environment. They're summarized on pages 53-55.

This list of core values isn't complete—nothing involving volunteer leadership is ever truly the last word. But it's a solid start, and we'd suggest you copy these core values and post them where you'll see it often. (For a convenient, abbreviated version see page 98.) It's where you're headed. And if you can, as a church, embrace these principles, you'll find most of the obstacles you're encountering melt away. Couple these principles with the skills and techniques of sound volunteer leadership, and you'll get where you need to go.

Core Values of Volunteer Leadership

In light of best practices with volunteers and our own experiences as volunteers, we hold these truths to be truly important—and hopefully self-evident:

Every volunteer experience in the church should encourage a healthy relationship with Jesus.

If that's not a natural outcome of a volunteer experience, either the volunteer has been misplaced in a role or the role isn't one that belongs in the church.

We believe everyone in the body of Christ has something to give to the corporate body.

Volunteer leadership cooperates best with the discipleship and stewardship process by honoring the abilities, interests, and passions of volunteers. We'll take the time to thoroughly discover volunteers and see that they're placed appropriately.

Volunteers are respected as full partners in ministry.

That means we lead volunteers in the same ways we lead paid staff members. Expectations about time may differ, but the standards of behavior and excellence are the same.

Volunteers can be any age.

Adults, teenagers, children—there's room for everyone to volunteer in a meaningful role, doing meaningful ministry.

(continued on next page)

It's better to leave a volunteer position unfilled than to put the wrong match in the position.

We will place volunteers in accordance to their abilities, interests, and passions, not based on our need to get someone to fill the slot.

We provide the resources and training that volunteers need to be successful.

Volunteers can expect to receive careful screening, thorough interviews, accurate position descriptions, and exemplary training and evaluations.

It's okay for potential volunteers to say "no" to a request.

We view a "no" as an invitation to explore alternative opportunities for involvement, not a sign of a potential volunteer's spiritual immaturity.

Volunteer motivation and retention are outcomes of doing other things right.

Among those things are:

- Valuing relationships and celebrating them.
- Valuing experiential training for volunteers.
- Valuing applicable training for volunteers.
- Valuing learner-centered training for volunteers.
- Fostering an environment where there's no put-down humor or victims and where volunteers can count on a culture that's fair, forgiving, and fun.

Volunteer leadership happens best when there's a centralized volunteer leadership function.

Few churches have a designated person to champion volunteer leadership. While that's the reality, it's not the ideal situation. We will provide resources to support the *function* of volunteer leadership, yet also encourage the emergence of the volunteer leader *role* in a church setting.

Episodic volunteering is legitimate.

Serving in a church setting doesn't have to be an "until death do us part" proposition. We recognize that volunteers may choose to volunteer in one role forever, or switch roles with some frequency. They may be available to volunteer at one stage of their lives and not at another. We'll honor any sort of appropriate service they're prepared and willing to do while fulfilling the needs of the congregation.

We won't let volunteers burn out.

They're too valuable and precious to use up and toss away. We value people serving well over a lifetime more than we value covering tasks.

The good of a local congregation supercedes the good of an individual volunteer.

The desire of a volunteer to serve in a specific area doesn't necessarily mean that's where the volunteer should serve. The corporate good of the ministry comes first in placing volunteers.

And we admit it: We can't motivate volunteers.

Though we can't motivate anyone, we *can* create environments where people experience motivation. Our goal is to "unlock" the innate motivation in individuals as we put in place those values, policies, and procedures that create "volunteer-friendly zones"—places where the culture is fair, fun, forgiving, and faithful. Where truth, trust, and clear expectations pave the way for communication success. Where direct communication is the norm and truth is spoken in love.

Obstacles to a Volunteer-Friendly Culture

The core values represent the attitudes and behaviors you want to see in your church. They summarize what a volunteer-friendly culture looks like at a practical level.

Now, what specific things might trip you up as you seek to build an effective volunteer-equipping culture? Where are the obstacles?

No two churches face precisely the same obstacles. Each church—yours included—is in a unique situation. You may have the issue of having too few people to fill ministry roles. Another church has too many people for one area of ministry, while it's short of people in another area. A church of 50 members has a very different set of challenges than a church of 5,000 members.

You may have a budget that's too small, and another church might have—believe it or not—a budget that's too big. Either can derail volunteer involvement.

Here's one church profile to consider...

The Church With Too Much Money

The church building is a majestic stone structure, with steeples making it visible from the entire inner-city neighborhood. The once fashionable streets surrounding the church building have fallen into disrepair over the past 50 years, and what was once a wealthy community has become a needy community. Substantial homes have been divided into apartments and flats. And aside from a few convenience stores tucked into storefronts, merchants have long ago gone out of business or moved to a "safer" neighborhood.

But the church building is immaculate. Every brick has been scrubbed clean of gang graffiti, and an armed guard patrols the perimeter each night. The parking lot is freshly sealed, and not one pane of glass is broken or covered with wire.

It's as if the church property has been frozen in time. It may be a depressing, decaying new millennium outside the church fence, but inside it's 1951.

When a consultant went into the building for a tour, he was greeted by an associate pastor who proudly showed him through the facility.

The sanctuary, which seated more than a thousand in carved wooden pews, smelled of fresh wood wax. The Christian education wing held more than a dozen classrooms, each with tiny tables and chairs in perfect rows. The nursery was spacious and newly carpeted.

All for a congregation of 32 people, with an average age of 67.

The associate pastor explained that on Sunday mornings the congregation enjoyed tremendous choral music—students from the nearby university's College of Music were under contract to sing and play. And another student was hired to sit in the nursery, on call to take care of any baby whose family came to visit.

No baby had been in the nursery for more than two years.

And the classrooms? Each week they were dusted and cleaned, but there was no Christian education program because there were no children—they'd graduated the last child out of the children's ministry department 15 years earlier.

What kept the doors open? An endowment funded by bequests in wills guaranteed that the building would always be kept in tip-top shape. The halls might echo when a visitor walked through on Sunday morning, but the floors were always perfectly waxed.

> The church knew it was in trouble.

The church knew it was in trouble. It needed to attract visitors, preferably from the neighborhood, so a volunteer leadership consultant was asked to make that happen. He'd be well paid to put together community events that would bring people into the building and, hopefully, into the church.

But because of their advanced age and busy schedules, none of the church staff or members of the congregation expected to be involved. The consultant could hire help as he saw fit from temp agencies or through the university student union office.

The consultant refused the assignment.

A huge budget had choked off volunteer involvement in this church because they could afford to pay others to do everything. In this case, too much money was a bad thing.

Assuming a bottomless budget isn't an obstacle in your way, what *are* the obstacles you're facing?

"A huge budget had choked off volunteer involvement in this church because they could afford to pay others to do everything."

Obstacles tend to fall into one of three categories:

1. Staff members who resist volunteer involvement,
2. Volunteers who resist serving, and
3. Inadequate volunteer leadership.

Let's look at these one at a time and ways we can approach overcoming them.

Why Leaders Resist Volunteer Involvement

- **Leaders have had a poor experience with volunteers.**

  The volunteers were late. They didn't do what they were asked to do. They didn't follow the rules. They were more interested in talking with each other than in finishing the work. The list of what constitutes a "poor experience" goes on and on.

  The obvious questions to ask would be what happened and whether it was specific to a particular volunteer or was caused by the design of the role a volunteer was filling.

And what might keep the experience from being repeated?

Work through the issues with leaders, and encourage them to approach future volunteer encounters with an open mind. If a leader simply won't work with volunteers, don't place volunteers with that leader. Let the success of the program in other ministry areas slowly change the leader's opinion of volunteers.

- **Leaders fear they'll lose their positions.**

  There *is* something awkward about having a former administrative assistant from a successful business helping out a church secretary who isn't a stellar administrator. Sometimes volunteers do a job so well that people begin to joke that the leader being helped isn't really needed anymore. Everyone laughs—except the leader.

  An insecure leader can create tremendous problems for volunteers, so discuss with leaders the benefits of using volunteers. The leader will be able to actually grow in his or her position because some tasks that formerly required attention will be handled by volunteers. Help the leader see the involvement of volunteers as an opportunity, not a threat. Assure leaders that volunteers will report *to* them and aren't being brought in to replace them.

- **Leaders fear the volunteers will make them look bad.**

  Perhaps it's fear that a retired principal who wants to help with the children's ministry will question decisions made by the children's pastor. Or that a board member who's helping with the ushering will tell the board that ushers really aren't needed and the group should be disbanded.

  Encourage these leaders to welcome input from volunteers and to think of them as full partners in ministry. Encourage volunteers to be sensitive to the roles of their leaders and to support those leaders.

- **Leaders fear volunteers are unreliable.**

  This is a realistic fear—some volunteers *are* unreliable. Share with leaders the processes for screening, training, and orientation that should be conducted with volunteers. Ask that the leader give volunteers a chance—and do your best to place reliable people in that leader's area.

- **Leaders want to recruit their own volunteers.**

  This is the system at place in many churches—each ministry area is responsible for its own staffing. In many respects, the system works well. An area ministry leader has a good understanding of the sort of person who will fit and be successful.

  In a centralized system of volunteer leadership, it's *still* the leader of a ministry area who does the final interview and determines if a volunteer will be placed in that area.

  But there's a potential problem when each ministry does its own recruiting. Some leaders just aren't very good at recruiting, and they're perpetually short of volunteers, while another ministry area is abundantly staffed. The children's pastor who is recruiting only for his or her ministry area may not know about positions in youth ministry or the choir; his or her filter for who will make a "good volunteer" is someone who fits in the children's ministry area.

  Unfortunately, this approach sabotages the overall volunteer program and builds resentments in areas where leaders aren't able to recruit effectively. Assure leaders that no volunteer will be placed in his or her area without that position being offered by the leader. No leader will be "stuck" with someone.

- **Leaders don't want to bother with supervising volunteers or completing the necessary job descriptions.**

  Unfortunately, both responsibilities come with having volunteers involved. If a leader refuses, politely offer to help create the position descriptions and to provide training for the volunteers. If the leader still refuses, don't place volunteers with that leader. Let the success of the program in other ministry areas influence this leader. Encourage peers who are using volunteers successfully to share their stories with this leader.

- **Leaders believe that using volunteers creates more work than it's worth, and they aren't rewarded for using volunteers.**

  Two issues are reflected here: the cost to leaders of supervising volunteers and the importance of volunteers being in ministry.

  Discuss with leaders that it's *worth* paying a price to involve people in ministry. In the same way that it's important to let children "help" at tasks until they master them, it's worth helping volunteers master tasks. Why? Because then the body of Christ has fully functioning members who are serving others and glorifying God in service. Encouraging that is one of the primary responsibilities of leadership in the church. Working with volunteers needs to be seen as a primary part of the leadership's responsibility and rewarded as such.

> ...it's *worth* paying a price to involve people in ministry.

Do this to get a discussion going: Suggest that equipping volunteers become a part of each staff member's job description for the reasons discussed above.

Staff objections to volunteer involvement fall into two general arguments: those borne out of experience and those fueled by fear.

If a staff member has truly had a negative volunteer experience, explore it in detail. Help the staff member determine how much of the problem was due to the volunteer, and how much was contributed by the staff member. What safeguards do you have in place—or *will* you have in place—to keep the same sort of situation from developing again? Sometimes just your continued involvement to monitor the staff member/volunteer role fit is enough to gain support.

But realize this: You can't *force* a volunteer on a staff member. If a specific staff member refuses to work with volunteers, that's a reality of your world. Work with the staff members who are willing to work with you, and encourage *them* to do the work you can't do: changing the hearts and minds of their peers.

Why Volunteers Resist Serving

Why do people refuse to become actively involved? Why do Pewsitters decide that a life of disengagement—which is boring and not consistent with their purpose in the church—is preferable to finding a place to serve? Again, the obstacles are numerous, but in my experience here are the most common obstacles you'll need to overcome:

- **"There aren't any jobs I can do."**

  When your potential volunteers see programs being delivered with excellence, the potential volunteers tend to focus on their own limitations. They see outstanding musicians leading singing, top-notch teachers doing children's ministry, smiling ushers greeting everyone like long-lost friends—it's daunting.

  Communicate to potential volunteers that there's training for any role they think suits them and that you'll only place volunteers where they have God-given strengths.

- **"I filled out one of those time and talent sheets and nobody called me."**

  All too often churches collect information about members and then promptly do...nothing. A volunteer interview process tightens up that loop and removes the possibility of inaction.

  What you don't want is to let a time and talent sheet officially reject people's gifts once a year. At an Equipping Institute conference, a lovely, silver-haired lady told us this sad story:

  "My husband passed away, so I moved here about a year and a half ago to live with my daughter. One of the first things I did was join a church. When I joined, they asked me to fill out a form listing my interests and talents and how I'd be willing to serve. I wrote down a long list because I was very active in my old congregation and now had lots of time on my hands. I was also eager to feel like I belonged in my new church family. It's been a year and a half and nobody has ever called to ask me to do anything. It makes me very sad."

Filling out paperwork doesn't place potential volunteers in fulfilling positions. We do that. Whatever paperwork we use is just a tiny first step in the process.

- **"I was so frustrated last time that I'll never volunteer again."**

  Here's a little secret: Many of those "frozen chosen" Pewsitters *have* been volunteers in the past. They didn't quit because they got too busy or too old or too anything. People don't easily quit things they find personally rewarding.

  They quit because they were in poorly defined roles, and they lacked the resources or authority to be successful. The problem wasn't with the volunteers—it was with the system in which they volunteered.

  Again—a volunteer interview program eliminates most of the opportunity for frustration because before a position is offered to a volunteer, that position has a ministry description in place, as well as a structure that provides evaluation and support.

- **"I hated my volunteer job."**

  Bad volunteer experiences happen to good people for a variety of reasons. Sometimes it's the fault of the volunteer—he or she isn't really committed or isn't able to give the time and energy the role requires. If the volunteer misrepresented what he or she was willing or able to do, that's going to create tension and failure.

  But sometimes the problem was that the volunteer was dumped on by a leader. By that, I mean the task given wasn't really delegated, it was dumped.

  The difference is this: If a leader thoughtfully thinks through how to share his or her work and hands off a task with the necessary resources and authority—that's delegation. If the task is something the leader *meant* to do but ran out of time and then in desperation handed it off—that's dumping.

Nobody likes to be dumped on...and few people will stick around to have it happen twice. When a volunteer has been delegated a task, that allows the volunteer to do ministry. But when a task has been dumped—that feels like anything *but* doing ministry.

> Nobody likes to be dumped on.

And sometimes volunteers disliked the roles they were in because they were in the wrong role all along. The volunteer soldiered along either until the results were so poor the volunteer was asked to leave or he or she was so miserable he or she quit.

A volunteer interview process offers the best opportunity to make a good fit for each volunteer, to get each person into the right job.

- **"Nobody seemed to care about me—or my ideas."**

Church leaders need to admit it: Sometimes we've made filling slots the goal, not placing the right person in the right job. We're handed a list of sixteen slots to fill on the organizational chart, and that's our focus. As long as someone is willing to let us write down his name, that's good enough for us.

Then we're off to fill the next chart.

There's no training. No follow-up. No evaluation. Little communication.

Who wants to work in a place like that—especially since volunteers don't have to do it? Sooner or later, people leave, and they're not inclined to come back. We haven't communicated that we care about people.

And when it comes to caring about people's ideas, there are two things we should never, ever say: "We don't do it like that here" and "But this is the way we always do it here." Those are two of the most demotivating phrases we can utter.

The message with either phrase (and attitude) is that we don't need your ideas, that we're happy with the status quo.

Here's a key point: Volunteers don't care whether you actually implement their ideas. They're happy when you do, of course, but it's not essential.

What *is* essential is that you actually *hear* the volunteer's idea and communicate respect for the idea and the volunteer who suggests it.

- **"I don't have time."**

  We all have the same amount of time in a day, a week, and a year. The issue isn't a lack of time, but that the volunteer opportunity being presented isn't important enough to rate a time commitment. We all make time for what we value most. Often the real issue is something else.

- **"I feel awkward talking about myself."**

  Under the best of circumstances, it's difficult for church members to tell us what they can do and what they can't do. It feels like bragging to point out one's strengths, and few people like to admit to weaknesses.

  So potential volunteers wistfully wish they could be given a role that actually fits them—but it's never offered. And it's never offered because we don't know to offer it. Instead, we offer roles that volunteers either try and hate or wisely refuse to take at all.

  It's also hard for church members to tell us what they're *tired* of doing. That feels like giving up or not being faithful. Here's a story that illustrates this point...

  A young woman joined a church and volunteered to help out in the Sunday school. She had a strong background working with junior-highers, so she was asked if she'd teach that age level. She agreed, and one Sunday morning she was walked up the stairs to where that class met.

  Here's what she saw as she came through the door: a tired man reading aloud from the book of Judges. He'd been working his way through the Old Testament, reading it aloud, as his three students suffered along.

  One student was busy scratching the varnish off the table with his fingernail. Judging from the almost total lack of varnish left, he'd been at it a while.

The second student was gazing out a window.

The third student was sound asleep.

The new teacher was introduced, and the man leading the class looked up in surprise. He shook her hand, closed his Bible, and walked out the door without saying a word.

It wasn't until later that the new volunteer found out the man had asked three years earlier if he could be relieved of duty. He didn't want to teach junior-highers any longer; he wanted to transport elderly people to church from nursing homes. *That's* where his passion was.

And the boy who was sleeping? That was the man's son.

A final thing we fail to hear from volunteers: what they would like to learn. What skills they'd like to develop. What talents they want to explore. Those places are where their interests lie—but we never get to tap into that fountain of motivation and enthusiasm. Why? Because we don't directly ask.

Why Do You Call People Who Serve "Volunteers"?

Perhaps it's not appropriate to call someone who is supposed to serve (remember our three theologies: *everyone* is called into significant ministry) a "volunteer," but that's the term we've chosen to use.

Some churches use other words to describe people who fill roles in the church. "Minister" and "servant" are among terms that some churches feel more accurately describe a Christian's role, considering that all believers are instructed to make available their God-given abilities, skills, and passions for service in the body of Christ.

Our research has shown, though, that only the word "volunteer" was widely recognized by most people in a congregation. An announcement asking for "ministers" to participate in a service role may leave some lay people thinking that only those with seminary degrees need apply.

In our Google-search society, "volunteer" is also the term most recognized for a person who serves without remuneration. It's why we use this word for some of our equipping ministry resources.

If you do choose to avoid the word "volunteer," consider simply referring to all people in volunteer roles as "unpaid staff." A Sunday school teacher would be a children's ministry unpaid staff member; a parking lot attendant would be a hospitality ministry unpaid staff member.

The word "staff" signals that every role is valuable and invites volunteers to think of their work as meaningful and on a par with pastoral staff and other paid individuals. It respects their full significance in ministry, but again, it may create confusion in the minds of potential volunteers.

Why Inadequate Volunteer Leadership Can Be an Obstacle

This last category of obstacles is all about us—the leadership and administration issues *we* bring into the equation.

Nobody wants to rearrange the deck chairs on a sinking ship. It's meaningless. When a ship is floundering, what people want most is to find a way *off* the ship. Everything else is busywork.

What's the reputation of your church when it comes to volunteers? Are you perceived as a sinking ship or a ship that's sailing along toward important places? When you run your mission up the center mast, do people salute?

When we ask volunteers to do things that aren't central to the mission of our church, we're providing inadequate leadership. When we ask volunteers to sign up for roles without giving them the information they need, we're providing inadequate leadership. And when we put volunteers in roles that don't suit them, we shortchange volunteers. It's easy to commit each of those sins, and each sin helps sink our reputation.

The fact is, we can be our own worst enemies when it comes to working with volunteers. What we say, what we do—in spite of our best intentions, we can easily create systems that make getting and keeping volunteers difficult.

You're clearly ready and willing to do your best to create a culture and structure where it's easy for people to embrace their God-given abilities, skills, and passions, and use those in ministry.

None of us will ever lead volunteers perfectly any more than we'll ever be a perfect follower of Christ. There will always be room for improvement and growth.

But you're growing—and God will bless and multiply your growth.

Let's look at three obstacles we may be throwing in our own way…

1. "I'll do it alone."

If you feel like a lonely voice crying in the wilderness, you're in trouble for two reasons. First, you're in the wilderness. You won't get much done there.

Second, nobody is listening to you. You're alone.

If you're the sole owner of the volunteer process in your church, the first thing you need to do isn't recruiting volunteers to fill the bell choir. The first thing you need to do is recruit people who'll share your vision and be your co-laborers.

You *cannot* run a volunteer-equipping process alone. It's too challenging and time-consuming. The work is never done. The phone calls never end. You must find some help. A team will provide you not just extra hands and feet but also morale-building and support.

If you're a person who thinks you've got to do it yourself to get it right, think again. Practice what you're preaching and recruit a team…even if you don't think you need one. *Especially* if you think you don't need one!

2. "I'm relying on spiritual inventories."

Perhaps you've tried to determine where your congregation is concerning volunteer ministry by using a spiritual gifts inventory. We applaud you if using a gifts inventory, or a time/talent survey, has actually increased your membership's level of service and involvement.

Frankly, that's often not the case.

In many churches where inventories are administered, they don't result in the actual placement of people in meaningful ministries. Why? Because there's no system of volunteer referral to connect people with volunteer roles. Too often church members are left frustrated as they think, *Now I know my spiritual gift—but what do I do with it?*

If you want to use spiritual inventories and surveys, wonderful…but here are some shortcomings that tend to create issues.

- **They're based on self-reporting.**

  People describe what they're like, and that often provides a skewed view of their skills and abilities. We often see ourselves as more or less gifted than we really are. Sometimes we don't have a realistic view of our own abilities at all.

  One way to remove this shortcoming is for each person who completes an inventory to have three or four close friends complete the same inventory *about* that person. It greatly increases the amount of work involved, but you'll get a clearer view of the person. If Brian sees himself as a gifted administrator but his wife and two friends see just the opposite—that's good to know.

- **Churches don't act on information gathered.**

  One church went to the expense and trouble of having every adult member complete a survey. The surveys were forwarded to the church office where they were carefully tabulated, collated, and filed away. When volunteer roles opened up in the church the leaders of those ministries skimmed through the surveys looking for a match.

  The problem was that people who were interested in volunteering had already done so—and not necessarily within the church. The local Habitat for Humanity and Salvation Army offices received lots of volunteers after the survey was given. Why? Because after several months passed without hearing from the church leadership, potential volunteers assumed that they weren't needed at church—so they looked elsewhere.

  If you've ever offered a personal gift to someone who unwrapped it, yawned, and tossed it aside, you know how it feels to fill out a time and talent sheet and have nothing happen as a result. It becomes a process of systematic rejection.

  This is what happened to a volunteer we'll call Audrey. Her experience isn't uncommon.

  Audrey was new to her church, St. Peter's, and didn't yet feel fully comfortable or accepted. It's not all the fault of the church—Audrey is a shy person who likes to be part of things but doesn't always know how to go about joining in. So by temperament she was stuck a little on the outside but wanting in.

Then one day a letter came. The Stewardship Committee had sent out the annual form, and Audrey was in a quandary. Deciding how much money to give was no problem, but she agonized over the time and talent portion of the form. Did she have time to share? Yes...but she wasn't sure she had any talent.

But she wanted to give more than money—by signing up to serve in a ministry area she'd get involved, become part of the group. She'd be known and accepted.

Audrey lay awake for hours agonizing over what boxes to check. What if she tried something and failed? What if she checked the wrong box? What if she really didn't have any talents?

In the morning she reviewed the list again, and after prayer and nail-biting she checked two boxes: typing in the office and helping with kindergarten in Sunday school. She felt a small thrill of anticipation as she tucked the list in her Bible, and an even larger thrill when the next Sunday she laid her form on the altar.

Stewardship Sunday had come, and at last she'd stepped forward to volunteer.

She waited for the phone to ring. She waited...and waited...

She's waiting still, and two more Stewardship Sundays have come and gone. She no longer places an "X" in any of the boxes.

Even if you act on information given, we strongly urge you to do one-on-one interviews with people. You'll discover a wealth of information that you won't find in any other way.

- **There's no personal interview to discover deeper information.**

  Okay, so a potential volunteer is a talented professional musician. The volunteer has received tremendous ovations time and again. Music is a passion, a talent, and, as far as the potential volunteer is concerned, a curse. After 20 years of playing music nonstop, the person would rather do *anything* than play one more note.

> Interviews reveal attitude, interest, and enthusiasm.

A gift inventory might well indicate that this person would make a perfect worship leader, and were the volunteer's attitude different, that's true. But the test won't reveal that the volunteer will take any other role before being condemned to do on Sunday what he does every other day.

Interviews reveal attitude, interest, and enthusiasm. Don't skip this step—it's a powerful tool in placing volunteers where they'll thrive.

3. "I'll get through this crisis, then start to do it right."

Think this and you'll just stay on the treadmill for another round.

Let's say someone hands you a list of "church jobs" to fill so programs can keep running. Maybe you've got a shopping list of three ushers, two committee heads, and a choir director. You fill those slots with willing people, but now you've got another five people who may be in the wrong positions. You haven't got the foggiest notion if they're going to thrive in their new jobs, or wither and die there.

There's no end to crises if you've got people in the wrong positions. It's like being in the eye of a hurricane: You can walk outside to see how bad the damage is and what's still standing, but you know the second half of the storm is coming. There's always another crisis on the way.

May we suggest this: If you haven't got time to do proper volunteer placement now, you'll never have time. That's because you're creating future disgruntled volunteers, unhappy volunteer managers, and an environment that's toxic for volunteerism.

Your intentions may be good—but your actions aren't. You're not following a key concept of volunteer leadership: *People are more important than programs.* That sounds simple, but it has some huge implications.

- **We won't sacrifice people so programs can continue.**

  If there aren't enough volunteers to staff the nursery properly, we declare the nursery off-limits until we have sufficient volunteers in place. That may sound radical, but think of what will happen if you have two worn-out volunteers caring for 23 infants. Not only is it unsafe, but you'll lose the two volunteers you have.

- **We won't think of "volunteers" as a unit, but as a collection of unique individuals.**

  If you don't know the names of volunteers who serve in your ministry area, how will you help them feel welcome? How will you know how to thank them? How will you be able to help them grow in their service? May the words "Let's leave that to the volunteers" never again be spoken in your church. Rather, let us hear words like "That sounds like something Frank, Tim, and Lenora would do well."

- **Ministries—even long-standing ones—may for a time be discontinued.**

  If you think starting a church program is hard, try stopping one that's become a tradition. It will seem like you're pulling the life-support plug on a loved one. But if there aren't enough organ-playing volunteers who stand ready to maintain and play the pipe organ, maybe it's time to give it up, at least for a while.

In the following survey let's quickly summarize the attitudes and behaviors we've identified as contributing to a toxic environment for volunteerism.

Attitude and Behavior Survey

Check each box you think applies to our church as you experience it. Please check boxes on the basis of what we *actually* appear to believe and do, not what we *should* believe and do.

- ☐ **Leaders don't truly believe that God has called each believer to do significant ministry.**
- ☐ **Leaders don't truly believe each believer has a God-given ability, skill, or passion to use in ministry.**
- ☐ **Leaders don't truly believe that each believer has a place where he or she fits into the body of Christ.**
- ☐ **Team leaders end up doing almost all the work on their teams.**
- ☐ **A handful of people (the church Pillars) do most of the work while others (the Pewsitters) watch.**
- ☐ **Leaders are asked to cover several major jobs at once—and keep those jobs too long.**
- ☐ **Leaders require unrealistic time commitments that scare volunteers away.**
- ☐ **There's no organized system for coaching volunteers.**
- ☐ **Volunteers are more committed to a leader than to the church.**
- ☐ **Clergy and other leaders fail to delegate to volunteers.**
- ☐ **Leaders are hesitant to work with volunteers because of a poor experience in the past.**
- ☐ **Leaders fear they'll lose their positions.**
- ☐ **Leaders fear the volunteers will make them look bad.**
- ☐ **Leaders think volunteers are unreliable.**

- ☐ **Leaders want to pick their own volunteers.**
- ☐ **Leaders don't want to bother with supervising volunteers or completing the necessary job descriptions.**
- ☐ **Leaders believe that using volunteers creates more work than it's worth and that they aren't rewarded for using volunteers.**
- ☐ **Volunteers don't think there are jobs they can do adequately.**
- ☐ **The church doesn't follow up on spiritual gift inventories or time and talent sheets.**
- ☐ **Frustrating volunteer experiences aren't debriefed and resolved.**
- ☐ **Volunteers have been placed in inappropriate jobs.**
- ☐ **The church is perceived as unresponsive to volunteers' suggestions.**
- ☐ **Volunteers feel uncomfortable talking about themselves at our church.**
- ☐ **Ministry leaders prefer to accomplish tasks on their own.**
- ☐ **It's perceived as too big a challenge to change the existing system of volunteer placement—even if it's inadequate.**

What are other attitudes and behaviors that affect volunteers and serving in our church but aren't noted above? Jot them below:

- ☐ ______________________________
- ☐ ______________________________
- ☐ ______________________________
- ☐ ______________________________

I am: paid church staff member_____ volunteer_____

Now glance at the boxes you and others have checked. Those are your prayer list. Ask God to work in the hearts of his people to change those attitudes and behaviors and to give you patience as you identify and deal with those attitudes and behaviors in others.

Also, pray that God uses you to help his people find appropriate places of service and experience joy in serving. You'll be cooperating with God's purposes as you assist in this ministry—may you find joy, too!

You know where you are—there are strengths in your church and weaknesses when it comes to serving and the use of volunteers.

But where are you going? What's your destination?

May we suggest: You want—you *need*—a volunteer leadership system built on solid biblical theology and solid volunteer leadership principles. Your next step is to catch a vision for a future that has that system in place.

5 Defining Your Future

Use this 12-step process for getting you where you want to be: enjoying a healthy, vibrant volunteer process that places the right people in the right jobs and serves everyone involved.

Okay, we've established that your church has some room for growth when it comes to encouraging more people to serve. That means you're just like every other church. We've yet to see a church that doesn't have room for growth.

So what are you going to do about it?

Let's begin by saying this: *No matter what obstacles you face, they can be overcome.* Don't be discouraged. You weren't asked to identify the challenges you face so they could stop you. We asked you to take a clear, realistic look at those challenges so you'll know how to proceed as you move forward.

In this chapter we'll outline a process that will be further developed. We'll briefly comment on the steps of the process so you can determine where you are at present and so you know what to do next.

But consider these cautions: *It's important you not skip steps.* You may have to adapt some of the steps to fit your situation (remember: *you're* the expert in your situation!), but each step has a definite purpose. It's like baking a cake: You can skip an ingredient as you mix the batter and at first it won't show, but once you've cooked the cake it will be obvious from the results that something was missing. This process is your recipe for volunteer equipping success. Don't skip any ingredients!

It's important you take these steps in order. You can't jump right to placing volunteers (step 8) before you set objectives and goals (step 3). This is a linear process, and each step builds on those before it. Like the core values, we suggest you make a copy of this process (a summary is on pages 91 and 92) so you can refer to it often. Hang it next to the core values list so you'll have a description of the culture you want to see created and the process by which you'll accomplish the following:

- You'll mobilize and energize more volunteers.
- You'll stop clergy and lay-leader burnout.
- You'll get the right people in the right ministries.
- You'll develop future leaders through effective delegation.
- You'll create a volunteer organization that's always being renewed and reinvented to stay current with trends that impact volunteerism in your community.

If that's the future you envision, let's get started!

The Volunteer-Equipping System: 12 Steps

The Volunteer Equipping System has been used in hundreds of voluntary organizations and churches. It's a centralized volunteer leadership system that brings about a "heart transplant" in organizations. That is, once it's in place it engenders a culture that's open to volunteers, and it encourages volunteers to grow in their service.

Let's review each step.

1. Establish a vision.

A vision answers the questions, "Where are we going?" and "Where does God want us to be in five years?" It's determining what we'd like our future to look like. We can just limp along hoping everything will work out, but that's neither proactive or powerful. Volunteers don't rally around the call of "Well, let's hope things don't get any worse."

Here's the truth: Without vision the people perish...and without vision a local *church* perishes, too. Not everyone is good at imagining the future and seeing where God is taking them. Not everyone is good at implementing things, either, or maintaining systems. Visioning requires a blend of skill, faith, and faithfulness to keep the vision grounded.

There often isn't anything terribly mystical about envisioning the future; it's doing some level-headed thinking about what truly is happening and what the implications are. Here's a story of how that can pay off for an organization…

John was delighted to discover, on a long airplane flight, that he was seated next to the Chief Planner of McDonald's. Since at the time John was the director of Colorado University's Graduate School of Business Management, he couldn't believe his luck. What a great opportunity to uncover some top-notch business techniques! John asked if he could pump the Chief Planner for insights to share with students, and the man agreed.

"But," warned the Chief Planner, "I'm not sure you'll believe how we do it."

John insisted anyway, and he quickly pulled out a pen so he could take notes on how one of the world's fastest-growing international companies did planning that carried them into the future.

The Chief Planner revealed that at the top of the McDonald's corporate headquarters in Chicago there was a special planning room. In the room was a skylight, a waterbed, and nothing else.

"Every department manager is required to spend one hour per week up there alone," said the Chief Planner. "The manager has to be on the waterbed, looking out the skylight. As the head of planning, I'm required to spend one hour per day up there. It's in my job description."

The Chief Planner continued, saying it was when he was on that bed, staring out the skylight, that the implications of zero population growth really hit him. This conversation took place during the years when the U.S. birthrate had declined and grade schools were being closed almost daily.

At that time McDonald's entire ad campaign was Ronald McDonald selling burgers and fries, and it was aimed squarely at kids. "We've got an entire planning department," the Chief Planner admitted, "and the population statistics were around...but nobody had put those statistics together with our future."

It was at that moment, on that bed, that McDonald's breakfasts were born. An entire diversification aimed not at children, but at adults.

You've got statistics, too. You know what's happening in your church and in your community. But have you put those together? Have you invited God to help you apply your creativity to the future—to take what the statistics tell you and to determine how you'll navigate those realities? To read a statistic and then ask "So what?" and "What if?"

> "Have you invited God to help you apply your creativity to the future..."

You need a vision for your church and your ministry. Begin with the church's vision, because the volunteer leadership vision must support that larger corporate vision.

2. Write mission and purpose statements.

Here's where you establish what business you're in—what problems you're trying to solve. If your mission is to present the Gospel to each person in your town, that's going to drive some of your decisions. It means you'll quickly fund an outreach in your community, but you might think twice about helping establish a seminary overseas.

If you're creating a mission or purpose statement for only your ministry area, you'll focus on how you can do children's ministry, youth ministry, or hospitality in such a way that you help the corporate church achieve its mission and purpose.

Start with your church's mission and purpose statements and be sure you support those. And if there aren't written church-wide statements, encourage the church leadership to create them. The outline at right will help them—or you—get started.

What is God calling you to be in this time and this place? The answer today as you're a church of 100 may change when you're a church of 1,000. As your neighborhood becomes more urban, or suburban, your mission may change. What's important is that you're deliberate and prayerful about stating it clearly.

How to Create a Mission Statement

1. Get the right people involved. Anyone who has a stake in the outcome should be involved in the process.
2. State WHY you exist—your purpose and what you want to accomplish. Keep the statement simple, and be honest and direct. Flowery prose has no place; you're writing to inform, not inspire.
3. Define WHO you want to serve. Who's your audience? Who should be paying attention to you?
4. Outline HOW and WHERE you'll get it done. Are you delivering goods and services? working with a specific group of people or in a specific location? Say so.
5. Remember your mission statement isn't being carved in granite. It will change as your organization changes.

3. Set objectives and goals.

To be useful, a goal must be written clearly and simply, and it must be specific. What *exactly* do you want to accomplish? Until you're specific, you can't determine if you've met the goal.

Make goals attainable. It doesn't do anyone any good if your goal is so lofty that nobody believes it can be reached. Who wants to give their best efforts to stretch for a goal that won't be reached anyway?

Make goals measurable every way possible, too. By time, certainly—decide when something needs to happen and put a calendar date on it—and also by number. If you need to schedule 12 appointments each month to place 6 volunteers, then create a goal of scheduling 12 appointments each month.

It's human nature for some of us to shy away from goals. We don't want to be locked in or fail to meet the goals. In the same way some sales professionals find goals motivating, some people find that goals suck the joy out of a task. Besides, when we're talking about "church stuff," how do you set a goal? When you tell God you want to see ten new children join the Sunday school, isn't that stepping over a line?

> Why not be specific about what you're trusting God to accomplish?

Setting goals is about focusing your energy and putting on paper what you trust God will do to and through you. You already know the goals you set are in accordance with what you've determined God wants to do in your church because your goals have flowed out of your mission. Why *not* be specific about what you're trusting God to accomplish?

4. Write an action plan.

Action plans are where you determine what steps will get you to each goal. Here's where you put wheels under each goal so you can move it forward from intention to reality.

Because your goals are specific, you've got a visual picture of the desired outcome for each goal. You know how to measure whether the goal has been successfully accomplished. You know where the finish line is.

Now it's time to think through how to get there. For each goal, write down the actions you may need to take to accomplish that goal. Don't worry about getting actions in order at this point—just write them down. It's not uncommon to find that a fairly simple goal ("paint the nursery") actually requires dozens of steps, so allow plenty of time—and paper!

Once you've exhausted your list-writing, then circle those that seem necessary and non-negotiable. The circled items will be your Key Action Steps. If there's a step that, with reflection, seems unimportant, lightly cross it off. This is the "analyze and prune" process.

Next, get organized. Place your circled Key Action Items in a logical sequence. What step has to happen first? second? Keep rearranging steps until you think you've got them in order. As you examine the list of Key Actions, are there any that could be simplified? that should be broken into several steps? that can be dropped altogether?

Get organized by estimating the amount of time each step will take and deciding who will be primarily responsible for each step. Accountability requires you to have each goal measurable in terms of time, budget, and people's performance, so keep those elements in place as you create an action plan.

It's wise to take your action plan even further by determining what resources you'll need to accomplish each step. By thinking it through on paper you may find that "painting the nursery" requires you to have scaffolding up for two solid weeks—which presents significant problems for Sunday child care. That piece of information will help you schedule the project for the least-disruptive time. And it lets you know that you'd better have the pastoral staff's input, too!

Move from the theoretical to the practical—to applying what you discover here to your unique church situation. Only you (and your team, if you have one) can create action plans for your church, because only you know all the factors that impact your possible actions. A course of action that makes great sense at one church might create more problems than it solves at another church.

5. Create position descriptions.

This is how you define the work to be done. It's also where you decide if the work will be done by paid staff or volunteers.

Written position descriptions are essential for sound volunteer leadership. It's no different than at a paid position: Without a job description there's no way to know what each person should be doing.

If you want to see what life without job descriptions is like, attend a pick-up volleyball game being played at a church picnic. Everyone knows what's supposed to happen—his or her team is supposed to knock the ball over the net in three hits or fewer. The ball is supposed to stay inside the boundaries drawn on the grass. You hit the ball back and forth until someone scores a point, and then you start over by serving the ball back into play. Simple.

So why is actually playing the game so difficult?

The answer is usually that while everyone has a *general* idea what to do, nobody is exactly sure what his or her *specific* job is. Balls land between players who thought it was someone else's job to hit the ball back. Someone in the back row mows over two players in an attempt to spike the ball from the front row. And players rotate positions, but nobody's quite sure when that's supposed to happen.

Chaos reigns on the court...and chaos can reign in your church, too.

When the assistant choir director takes it upon herself to change the order of service while the choir director is out of town, is that okay? Does she really have the authority?

If the volunteer janitor finds a leaking pipe one Friday afternoon, who does he call? Who's been deputized to call for a plumber?

And when there are two office assistants, whose job is it to fold all the bulletin covers—the job *nobody* likes to do?

Position descriptions answer those questions, and more besides. They nail down what duties the volunteer position includes, who the volunteer reports to, and how long the job will last. Position descriptions provide all the information a potential volunteer needs to know to make an informed commitment.

And if you'll go to the trouble to place your volunteer position descriptions on your church web site, you'll let potential volunteers have access to information about opportunities with just a few keyboard clicks. New members can see what jobs are already available—which often prompts inquiries about those jobs or jobs that aren't there but could be.

6. Recruit volunteers.

This step uses the "R" word. Everyone understands the concept of recruitment, but we admit, it doesn't describe the context. So the disclaimer is this: Recruitment, in the church setting, is really the process of inviting people into ministry.

Recruitment is an invitation to come discuss a volunteer role. It doesn't mean the person responding will necessarily get the position.

For many churches, this is a revolutionary approach to filling volunteer roles. Not everyone who signs up for a position automatically gets it.

Don't worry—being more selective about who you place as volunteers and more particular about where you place people doesn't hurt your ministry. It *helps,* as you'll discover that volunteers are happier, stay longer in their roles, and happily give positive testimonies about their volunteer participation.

If recruitment has become a necessary evil, or the least favorite of your responsibilities at church, we hope you're ready for a fresh perspective on placing people in volunteer jobs. When done right, it's a *ministry* that can bring about enormous spiritual growth in the lives of volunteers.

7. Interview potential volunteers.

You can't do a good job of placing people in volunteer roles without knowing about them...and actually *knowing* them.

Perhaps you use surveys to collect information. That's fine, but it's incomplete.

A quick word about this step in the process: It's where a tremendous amount of ministry can happen in the span of 25 or 30 minutes as potential volunteers are heard and encouraged. At church we're very good at transmitting information, and we're often excellent when it comes to providing inspiration. But there's less opportunity for people to be heard—honestly, deeply listened to—by another person.

By "inner-viewing" potential volunteers you'll provide that blessing. Plus, you'll be equipped to recommend the right volunteer roles to each potential volunteer.

8. Place volunteers.

How will you ensure that effective connections are made between volunteers and opportunities? The activities included in this step provide the critical link between the volunteer, his or her ministry leader, and the ministry area in which the volunteer will work.

Think of this as that last ten feet between the Space Station and one of the shuttles bringing astronauts to the Station. Everyone knows that the fittings on both vehicles will join together. There's no question that everyone is motivated for the "docking maneuvers" to go well. But no matter how far the astronauts have flown to get on board the Space Station, if they can't navigate that last ten feet and make contact, they're not getting aboard.

9. Train and support volunteers.

Getting the right person in the right job is just part of what it takes to have a successful volunteer ministry. You're not successful until the volunteer has become successful, too, and that takes training and support.

How will your church orient volunteers so they have the information they need and they feel comfortable? How will you equip volunteers with the skills they need to be effective? How will you provide support if problems arise?

It's wise for you to be asking those questions, because it's certain your potential volunteers are asking them!

The vast majority of volunteers want to do an excellent job in their volunteer role; it's important that we give them every chance to do so.

10. Recognize volunteers.

How will you thank volunteers for what they do? How often? Will you affirm and thank volunteers individually or by teams? Few people volunteer to be recognized, but many drop out because they weren't.

"Few people volunteer to be recognized, but many drop out because they weren't."

11. Supervise volunteers.

In the same way you expect to supervise paid staff, you need to supervise volunteers. This is especially important because volunteers generally *want* to be supervised. They *want* to get better at what they're doing. They view their volunteer jobs as important and significant. They need to know you feel the same way.

You may find that supervision includes...

Coaching—as you work with volunteers to create and track their performance against goals, action plans, and timelines. If you want to be able to delegate to volunteers, it's critical that you ensure volunteers are prepared to see the tasks and responsibilities through.

Serving as a liaison—as you help the volunteer understand the church's overall mission, goals, and policies. And, conversely, you help ministry leaders understand a volunteer's concerns.

Mentoring—as you help connect a volunteer with resources and experiences that will help the volunteer grow. Typically, it's the ministry leader to whom a volunteer reports that will fill this role, but there may be elements of mentoring in your relationships, too.

Your goal is to see that each volunteer is supervised appropriately. It's almost never appropriate for *you* to be doing direct supervision. That role will be filled by the ministry leader who directly supervises each volunteer—but you need to see that it happens.

12. Evaluate volunteers.

Most people hate being evaluated. We associate it with tests we've failed or annual meetings with a boss who has a long list of our failures to review. And because we dislike *being* evaluated, we're hesitant to *do* evaluations.

Your goal is to see that each volunteer supervisor is able and willing to evaluate volunteers in his or her area—and is equipped to do helpful evaluations, *positive* evaluations.

Generally, your contribution to the cause is to ensure that there's a clear position description for each volunteer job and that responsibilities are equally clear. And you must train into supervisors of volunteers the notion that performance reviews are an ongoing process, not a quarterly or annual matter. If an employee is willing to improve anytime throughout the year, why mention areas where improvement is needed just once every three months? Praise—and encouragement to grow—need to come far more often.

Make evaluations discussions with feedback rather than lectures and you'll find that volunteers actually *enjoy* them. And so will you.

There are two things you want to cover in a volunteer evaluation: *What are the volunteer's "well-dones"?* These are the things that a volunteer is doing well and that you'd love to see continued.

What are areas in which the volunteer could improve? We all have them, and sometimes we don't see them until someone gently points them out. That begins the process of feedback. Begin with the assumption that the volunteer genuinely wishes to be excellent in his or her service, and help the volunteer plan how to achieve excellence.

You may discover, in the course of an evaluation, that the volunteer isn't actually doing what's in his or her ministry description. Maybe the person initially came on board to lay out the monthly newsletter, but now that's done with a standard template. So the volunteer has been running the folding and stuffing machine instead. If there's a need to adjust a position description, the evaluation is a great place to do it.

Also, ask what would help volunteers better fulfill their roles and what resources are needed. Invite volunteers' suggestions about what might help your church better fulfill its mission and goals. What ideas do volunteers have for improving how things get done?

Volunteers' suggestions are worth their weight in gold, because volunteers see and hear things that will never reach your eyes or ears. Plus, giving volunteers permission to make suggestions removes the "I'm just a volunteer" mentality that keeps some volunteers from fully engaging.

> "Volunteers' suggestions are worth their weight in gold because volunteers see and hear things that will never reach your eyes or ears."

When you've got a homemaker, a Christian educator, and a mechanical engineer all volunteering in the nursery, they're seeing that experience from three very distinct perspectives.

The homemaker will suggest ways to make the nursery a warmer, more nurturing environment.

The Christian educator will find ways to use music and interaction with the babies to do teaching.

And the mechanical engineer will figure out a way to isolate dirty diapers in an airtight container within ten seconds of the diapers being removed from the babies.

They're all helpful contributions! Be sure you ask for those ideas—and that you empower volunteers to implement good ideas they generate.

How are you doing with these 12 steps of volunteer leadership? A little self-assessment can be healthy, so pause and fill out the chart on pages 91-92. Complete the form yourself, but first make photocopies of the chart. Give a copy to your pastor and other staff members (if there are any), and also to some of your volunteers. Then see how the answers provided by others compare to yours.

Also, chart how the answers of paid church staff compare to the answers of volunteers. Do your staff think volunteers have everything they need to be effective, but volunteers don't share that perception? If you find there's a discrepancy between how staff and volunteers perceive life, that's a great reason to go open up a dialogue with staff about why changes must be made in your current volunteer leadership process.

Volunteer Equipping Assessment Survey

	Not Done At All	Needs Improvement	Done	Done Well
Vision We have a clear idea where we're going, and that idea is shared by our entire church leadership.	☐	☐	☐	☐
Mission and Purpose We have a clearly articulated mission and purpose statement. We know what God wants us to be and do in this place, at this time.	☐	☐	☐	☐
Objectives and Goals We know specific things we wish to accomplish and why accomplishing those things will help us fulfill our mission and purpose.	☐	☐	☐	☐
Action Plan We know how we'll get things done, when, and who is responsible for results.	☐	☐	☐	☐
Position Descriptions We have written position descriptions for every volunteer role.	☐	☐	☐	☐
Recruitment We're inviting people to come discuss volunteer roles.	☐	☐	☐	☐

(continued on next page)

	Not Done At All	Needs Improvement	Done	Done Well
Interviews We have an established procedure (and trained interviewers) for conducting one-on-one interviews with potential volunteers.	☐	☐	☐	☐
Volunteer Placement We have an established procedure for matching volunteers with specific volunteer opportunities.	☐	☐	☐	☐
Training and Support We have a volunteer orientation program in place and training programs that provide significant, needed information to volunteers.	☐	☐	☐	☐
Volunteer Recognition We have a planned, intentional calendar of group recognition events and/or a system for recognizing volunteers individually.	☐	☐	☐	☐
Supervision We have a system in place that provides each volunteer with competent supervision that helps volunteers develop and grow in their roles.	☐	☐	☐	☐
Evaluation Each volunteer is evaluated on a regular basis.	☐	☐	☐	☐

6

How to Carry the Vision Forward

Two approaches for moving the vision for serving forward—one for pastors, one for other church leaders.

What you do next to turn the future you'd like to see—where serving is a natural and common part of your church's experience—depends on who you are. That is, the next step for a pastor is different from the next step for a Sunday school superintendent or youth leader. Here are some suggestions for both groups...

Next Steps for Pastors

If you're a pastor looking for a church-wide volunteer leadership system that will bring about transformational change:

- **Pray about it.** Your very next step is to pray daily about the direction you believe God is calling you. Urge other church leaders to pray, too. Is instituting a church-wide volunteer leadership system God's direction for your church right now?
- **Do your homework.** Have leaders and some of your existing volunteers (both active and inactive) fill out the Volunteer Equipping Assessment Survey (pp. 91-92) and Attitude and Behavior Survey (pp. 74-75). Summarize the data so you're ready to report what you discovered.
- **Schedule a meeting with stakeholders.** Invite volunteers, church leaders, everyone who might be impacted by changes in the volunteer equipping system. The purpose of these meetings is not to condemn or create guilt, but to gain insight into where you are now and where you want to be as a congregation.

  Begin your meeting(s) with devotions. Consider letting your devotions flow out of Scripture, perhaps these passages: Deuteronomy 1:9-15; 1 Corinthians 12:14-27; Ephesians 4:11-16; 1 Peter 4:9-11; or 1 Peter 5:1-3.

- **Prayerfully do some dreaming about your *what-ifs.*** Ask God to give you a clear and exciting vision for where you can be, and the impact you can have in your community. Prayerfully ask God to give you a vision that lines up with his will for your church, your membership, and his plans for your neighborhood and town. Humbly seek to accomplish God's purposes.

  If the vision that emerges is to have an equipping church culture throughout your ministry, then make it a priority to begin *now*...knowing it may take three to five years to accomplish such a church-wide change.

- **Select a task force to take responsibility for implementation.** Form a team to begin the process of becoming a church which celebrates the ministry of all Christ-followers. It may well be that you're not the right person to coordinate this effort. That's not a reflection on you personally; it's a recognition that as the pastor of your church you have other roles to fulfill. Plus, if the change is to be authentic throughout the church, having decisions made and implemented by lay people is essential.

  The final outcome in a few years may not be precisely what you envisioned, or accomplished in quite the way you'd have done it, but it will be in place and powerful. Your church will have ownership of the process. And it will be successful and working.

  Are you unwilling to trust your congregation to move ahead with something that's so important? After all, they're "just volunteers."

  By the way, if you're nodding in agreement with that last paragraph, please review the three theologies at the beginning of this book. Your church members certainly *can* be trusted to do significant ministry! God wired them for it!

- **Provide support and encouragement.** Your task force is going to hit some rough water along the way. It will be a wonderful contribution if you continually provide support for the project from the pulpit and in prayer.

Next Steps for Leaders

You're the leader of a ministry area, and you're looking to transform just your corner of the church. You'd like to change the entire congregation's view of volunteers and serving, but that's beyond the scope of your abilities. Fine-tune the process in only your own ministry area and you'll see results in the lives of your volunteers and the lives they touch.

Here's how to move ahead with implementing the volunteer equipping process in just the youth ministry area or Christian education area or wherever else you serve and lead.

- **Begin with prayer.** Shifting how volunteers are brought on board and retained just *seems* like a small thing—it's huge! The impact will be felt church-wide even if you have nothing to do with another ministry area.

  Volunteers will be treated differently in your piece of the organization. You'll do things for and with your volunteers that won't be part of every church volunteer's experience. You can expect to hear some questions about what you're doing and why. And you may discover that volunteers from other areas begin to migrate your direction.

  And that will very quickly be noticed by other ministry leaders.

How to Keep Anonymous Surveys Anonymous

You'll get more honest answers if survey responders trust that their responses will *truly* be kept anonymous—that you won't know who said what.

You can accomplish that by enlisting the help of a trusted person who is not closely associated with you. The pastor's secretary, for instance, or a trusted church layperson.

Along with the surveys, include a note directing respondents to return their surveys to that trusted person, who will compile the information, re-key all written comments in a separate document, and then destroy all original surveys—without showing them to you. Or use surveymonkey.com to send out the questions!

Prayerfully ask God for both guidance and grace. Be sure your motivation is for the good of the volunteers you serve, not to "show the pastor how it's done" or to rustle a few volunteers away from other ministry areas.

Pray daily for guidance regarding which functions in the 12-step Volunteer Leadership System will offer the most help to your program. (It's often Volunteer Ministry Position Descriptions and Interviewing.) Confirm this with your present volunteers. Be realistic.

- **Honestly fill out all the assessment tools in this chapter.** The Volunteer Equipping Assessment Survey (pp. 91-92) and Attitude and Behavior Survey (pp. 74-75) will give you huge insights—but not necessarily ones you enjoy. Ask some of your volunteers to anonymously fill out the surveys and compare their answers with your own. You may discover you don't understand life as volunteers in your church experience it.
- **Prepare spiritually.** Do personal or team devotions that flow out of some of the passages listed on page 93. Let God speak to you about how he wants to use his church to impact the world. (Deuteronomy 1:9-15; 1 Corinthians 12:14-27; Ephesians 4:11-16; 1 Peter 4:9-11; or 1 Peter 5:1-3.)
- **Watch for God's timing.** When you feel God's nudging, pursue one or two volunteer functions you want to add, or in which you want to improve volunteer participation.
- **Keep moving ahead—but not alone.** Remember, one of our goals is that you not burn out. Getting volunteers to help you in significant ways is key to that goal.

Let's review where you're at now—before moving forward.

- You've got your vision set and you know where you want to go.
- You've considered the three theologies that are the foundation of a biblical approach to volunteer leadership.
- You've decided it's worth dealing with the personal change that's going to be required.
- You have determined if your church is volunteer-friendly and have thought through how to deal with any issues that have arisen.
- You've defined your preferred future as you've worked through the 12-step process. You're ready to carry the volunteer program forward.

Now, let's get down to business.

Core Values of Volunteer Leadership

- **Every volunteer experience in the church should encourage a healthy relationship with Jesus.**
- **We believe everyone in the body of Christ has something to give to the corporate body.**
- **Volunteers are respected as full partners in ministry.**
- **Volunteers can be any age.**
- **It's better to leave a volunteer position unfilled than to put the wrong match in the position.**
- **We provide the resources and training that volunteers need to be successful.**
- **It's okay for potential volunteers to say "no" to a request.**
- **Volunteer motivation and retention are outcomes of doing other things right.**
- **Volunteer leadership happens best when there's a centralized volunteer leadership function.**
- **Episodic volunteering is legitimate.**
- **We won't let volunteers burn out.**
- **The good of a local congregation supercedes the good of an individual volunteer.**
- **And we admit it: We can't motivate volunteers.**

7 Getting Down to Business

What do you expect volunteers to accomplish in your church? And in which areas of ministry? Here's how great planning—and action plans—will help you nail down those details.

Let's imagine that a well-off, well-loved person in your congregation died a few months ago. A few weeks after the funeral, a lawyer visits your church office with some interesting information.

"Mrs. Anderson left five million dollars to the church," announces the lawyer, "but she stipulated in her will that this money be used for one purpose only: to fund several new staff positions for key ministry areas in the church."

Really? No problem!

Then the lawyer drops the other shoe: "There was one other stipulation: The new staff members have to be brought on board in 60 days and be successful in their positions for a year."

The odds are your church board would find a way to meet that evening in an emergency session. Inside a week there would be a plan in place outlining where the new staff positions would fit into the organization. Job descriptions would be written, advertising done, interviews arranged, and the new positions would be filled in 60 days—even if it took 18-hour days to fill the last opening.

During their first year the new staffers would receive ample training, get plenty of feedback and mentoring, and be compensated appropriately. They'd know exactly what they were doing well, what needed improvement, and how to go about meeting performance standards.

When that one-year anniversary rolled around and the lawyer came to see if he should sign over the check, he'd find a well-oiled, fully-functioning church staff. Why? Because there was tremendous motivation to see that each staff member had what was needed to be effective and successful.

The bad news is that you probably don't have a Mrs. Anderson waiting in the wings to give you five million dollars. But the good news is that you don't need her. If you'll go through the same careful, thorough planning process you'd go through to bring on paid staff and "hire" volunteers instead, you'll still accomplish an amazing amount of ministry.

> It's worth planning thoroughly for a volunteer role.

The point: It's worth planning as thoroughly for a volunteer role as it is a paid staff member's role.

We know planning is important. We've gone on vacations. We've survived building programs. We know that failing to plan wastes time, money, and energy, and can result in programs that are disappointing to the people we serve.

Are we planning carefully when it comes to our volunteers?

Even at first blush, it's easy to see that there are many places volunteers can do significant ministry in your church. Later in this book you and your core team will be pausing to look in detail at volunteer opportunities in your church (these are places volunteers *could* serve, not necessarily where they're *already* serving); for now let it be enough to see that you've just demonstrated the need for increasing volunteer involvement. You may have to demonstrate it again for your church's paid staff members.

By the way, since we're talking about both paid staff and volunteers, let's mention something to keep in mind as you and your core team move ahead in planning how to utilize more volunteers. If your church (or ministry area) has both paid staff and volunteers, it's important that you emphasize the importance of *both*. While volunteers aren't paid to carry out some aspect of ministry, God calls them to be ministers (see the three theologies discussed earlier) just as he calls those who make their paid profession "ministry."

The Five-Million-Dollar Phone Call

Imagine you've received a phone call from Mrs. Anderson's estate lawyer. You've got five million dollars to fund several new staff positions. What areas of ministry could use extra staff? Where would you spend the money to add staff?

Now, in those ministry areas, how might volunteers fill those same roles and accomplish those same tasks?

Make sure your volunteers feel like full partners in ministry, a vital part of your church's ministry team. Many of your volunteers are investing in the lives of others—caring for children in the nursery, teaching children in Sunday school or children's church, delving into relationships with middle schoolers and high schoolers, or helping adults grow spiritually in small groups

"Make sure your volunteers feel like full partners in ministry."

and Bible classes. Those efforts are vitally important ministry; don't communicate somehow that volunteers are less significant than paid staff members.

One way to help keep equity between paid and unpaid (volunteer) staff is to see that volunteers understand exactly why they're serving. They should agree with, and feel passion for, your church's or ministry's mission statement—as well as your goals and objectives.

Also, help volunteers understand that *you* see them as far more than unpaid labor. Interact with them as front line troops you trust entirely to invest in the lives of others.

You've determined some of the ministry areas in which volunteers could have an impact. Let's say one of those is the church office, where the pastor reports that chaos reigns supreme. It seems correspondence is always behind, the attendance record is six months out of date, and the sole paid secretary is overwhelmed.

You're determined to treat volunteers as full partners in ministry.

You're determined to treat volunteers as full partners in ministry, so your office volunteer will have all the training, tools, and information necessary to be effective. The volunteer will have a comfortable desk, reasonable hours, and an invitation to attend general staff meetings.

So what's next? Do you open the office door, throw a volunteer in, and hope the volunteer thrives? No...because you've still got work to do before your volunteer can hope to be useful and effective. The volunteer is needed...but you're not sure exactly how. You've got to do some planning.

Creating Action Plans

The idea of creating action plans is pretty simple—your core team decides *what* to do, *how* you'll do it, *when* you'll do it, and exactly *who* will do it. In the context of volunteer leadership, planning is when you decide what things you'll actually *do* to achieve your objectives—and those plans become action plans.

Looks simple, doesn't it?

It *is* simple—but so is moving rocks.

A friend once hired some workmen to shift some of the large boulders on her property so she could make better use of the land near her house. She and the foreman walked around the yard while she pointed to which boulders she wanted moved, and she pointed out exactly where she wanted them deposited. As she talked, the foreman carefully drew a map and drove stakes in the ground.

When they'd finished their stroll, our friend looked at the map the foreman had drawn and confirmed that the wooden stakes were in the right spots.

"That," the foreman said with a grin as he tucked the map in his pocket, "was the *easy* part." He knew from experience that actually shifting the stones was difficult. So difficult, in fact, that he didn't want to do it twice—so he took great pains to be sure there was a firm plan in place before the work started.

You need similar plans: careful, thorough, and shared with everyone who either has to do the work or deal with the consequences.

In short, you need action plans.

> You need action plans.

You need them for your general work as a ministry (for instance, you'll need to meet with paid staff to gather information) and you'll need to create action plans for individual ministry areas (for instance, you may identify the need for a church office volunteer to accomplish key tasks). Those action plans for individual volunteers are the beginning of a position description, and we'll deal with those in depth shortly.

Action Plans Defined

An "action plan" is where you determine specific steps to get you to each goal. You think through tactics and sequences of activities, what will happen and when, and what the budget will be.

Each of your volunteer ministry's goals needs a complete action plan, including (and we can't emphasize this enough) *to whom you are delegating the responsibility to achieve the goal.* (We'll explore *what* to delegate later in this book.)

Many voluntary efforts are launched for worthy causes, but they lacked a plan. People saw a need and decided to do something about it, but because they didn't plan how they'd tackle the problem or implement a service, their efforts flourished briefly and then faded.

Volunteers who signed on to help those causes felt burned, and probably thought twice before volunteering again. People who were going to benefit from the efforts had their hopes temporarily raised, then felt less hopeful than before.

Nobody emerged a winner.

Action plans would have helped those good causes determine how to not just start strong, but also to finish strong. And any shortfalls in money, time, or expertise would have become obvious before reaching a critical point. If you're going to run out of gas, it's good to know that before you're out on the highway.

Finding a Few Good Men—and Women

When you're creating and implementing a volunteer ministry action plan, be sure to choose people to help you who have some competence in areas related to the goal. You need more than just willingness. Enthusiasm can carry you just so far.

If you were planning to remodel the church kitchen, wouldn't you feel more comfortable if a plumber or an electrician were sitting in on the meeting? They bring practical knowledge to the table, and that can help you keep from making wonderful plans that have no hope of ever being implemented.

It's a balance as you ask your team to do planning with you. You want to have the enthusiasm of the uninformed ("Let's put the sink on an island in the center of the room—it will let more people help clean dishes") as well as the seasoned advice of the informed ("If we move the sink there, we'll have to put the plumbing straight through the pastor's study downstairs").

If you have experts on your team, people tend to quickly defer to them. There's less brainstorming and "possibility thinking." But in reality, you did most of that possibility thinking back when you were generating a vision and mission statement. Now it's time to zero in on your goals and be practical in how you'll achieve them.

Now it's time to zero in on your goals and be practical in how you'll achieve them.

Your planning team includes people who are representing constituencies, so give team members permission to speak on behalf of their groups as plans unfold. A church staff member may have almost no preference about how the kitchen is remodeled apart from the budget involved, but the hospitality committee representative (who knows the ins and outs of potluck dinners) will have a *lot* to say.

Remind task force members that their expertise and experience is valued as action plans are developed. Encourage people to speak their minds.

As part of your action planning (remember, you'll design an action plan for each goal), let the person(s) responsible for that area help define the details. You've got a task force of the right people pulled together, so let them take the wheel on this process. Remember: Most people are far more committed to plans *they* help make than to plans *you* made. A suggestion you make that might be quickly dismissed as impractical will often, if suggested by a task force member, be given careful consideration. Modifications will be made. Compromises reached.

And a notion that was initially thought impossible will eventually be transformed into a goal that's very reachable.

> Action plans are useful only if you follow through.

Action plans are useful only if you follow through and identify all the information you need…

Who will take responsibility for implementing the plan? You need a name. It may be a team or committee who completes the work, but you need the name of the person spearheading the effort.

How will the action be implemented? Be specific—break the action into steps that make sense and can be tracked.

When will each step be taken? Without a deadline you can't measure progress, so be specific.

The cost matters, too—especially if there are discounts or savings available if the plan is implemented in a timely fashion.

If you're a person who likes charts, those that follow might be helpful as you pull together your action plans. The first is bare-bones, and the second one on pages 108 and 109 allows you to plan in greater detail.

Action Plan for the Following Goal:

Who	How	When	Cost

Action Plan for the Following Goal:

Action Steps	Review Date	Risk	How to Measure Results

Obstacles Expected	Ideas to Avoid/ Lessen Obstacles	Our Success Confidence Level?

Know When You Should Plan

Knowing precisely when to do your planning can be tough in church settings.

Many ministries roll along full steam, burning through people, money, and time, yet without a clear definition of exactly what the ministry is supposed to be doing. Somehow, the ministry leaders never turned an overarching purpose into measurable goals and objectives.

This can also happen with new areas of ministry. Good people pull together to start a ministry to singles or to seniors. They jump in, but their lack of planning inevitably causes them to run into problems keeping support from church leadership, getting funds from the church budget, or even retaining the people they want to serve. Good volunteers get lost in the process. Potential volunteers don't see any promise for their own growth by being involved in a failing ministry. It becomes a mess because planning didn't happen in a timely fashion.

Clearly, it's not a good idea to do planning too late. But it's also not a good idea to plan early on, then quit planning. When should you plan? A short answer: *Always* be planning.

> "Planning needs to be an ongoing and constant process in your ministry."

Planning needs to be an ongoing and constant process in your ministry. That's one reason to loop the evaluation process back into the planning process. As you evaluate where you've been, you can see how needs have changed, workers have developed new interests, or your church has changed. As you evaluate and come up with new goals and objectives, you'll be aware of and responsive to those changes.

How to Write Action Plans

You can approach creating action plans in any number of ways, but here's a simple, four-step method. Let's briefly walk through the steps, then provide an example of how it looks in the real world.

Step 1. Prepare

- State your goals and objectives clearly and specifically.
- Collect facts, opinions, and the experience of others that may bear on the situation at hand.
- Consult with everyone who may be involved—directly or indirectly.

Step 2. Decide

- Analyze all the data you've collected, and think through possible consequences.
- Develop alternative courses of action.
- Evaluate the alternatives and choose the best one.
- Set standards.

Step 3. Communicate, Communicate, Communicate

- Determine who'll be affected by the action plan—directly and indirectly.
- Select and implement the best methods for communicating the action plan to those people.
- Check to be sure everyone understands and accepts the action plan.

Step 4. Control

- Set checkpoints to evaluate progress on the action plan—key dates and steps.
- Compare actual with anticipated results.
- Take remedial action when necessary (change the current plan or even change plans altogether).

Four steps—it looks easy on paper, but we all know how simple things can become complex when you start to add people. The good news is that even when you add people, this really *is* a straightforward process.

Let's take a look at how these planning steps might look in a volunteer ministry setting. Suppose a preschool director is considering adding volunteers from the church to help with a weekday preschool/daycare ministry. The volunteers will work alongside paid staff caregivers.

Now let's run through those four planning steps again…

1. Prepare.

- Goal: Add five volunteers from First Community Church to assist paid staff in preschool ministry.
- Check with state licensing board for limitations or restrictions on using volunteers, training requirements, and background checks required. Call other churches with similar programs to see if they use volunteers, and ask them to assess the strengths and weaknesses of volunteer involvement.
- Ask the preschool director and current paid staff to identify the busiest times of day when volunteers could help most.

2. Decide.

- Ask the preschool director, one or two present staff members, and the church's Christian Education Director to form a task force to help make decisions.
- The task force reviews data and information collected in Step 1 and weighs the pros and cons of using volunteers.

  Possible alternatives:

  (1) Recruit five volunteers who will assist for two-hour blocks, one each morning of the week, during the busy child-drop-off time (7 to 9 a.m.).

(2) Recruit ten volunteers who will assist for two-hour blocks, one each morning of the week, and one each afternoon of the week, during the busy child-drop-off time (7 to 9 a.m.) and child-pick-up time (4 to 6 p.m.).

(3) To meet state licensing requirements, volunteers will need intensive training. Before we invest in training a large number of volunteers, recruit two people and train them, and start a pilot program two mornings per week. Determine whether, because of licensing restrictions and requirements, a program using volunteers in preschool ministry will work at this time.

3. Communicate.

- The committee decides the best method for communicating the plan to potential volunteers and to others who are affected, such as staff or parents. Options for communication include a newsletter, group meetings, personal meetings and interviews, newspaper announcements, memos in children's diaper bags, e-mails, and posting on the church website.
- Once the final decision is implemented, the task force will make sure everyone is informed appropriately.

4. Control.

- The committee realizes that part of the original plan in step 2 should include evaluation. The task force will become an advisory board and continue to meet monthly. They'll ask for verbal or written reports from the preschool director to evaluate if the program is meeting agreed-upon objectives.
- The task force will develop written surveys that will be completed every six months by parents of preschoolers in the program and by the volunteers involved.
- If there are any problems, the preschool director can call a special meeting to determine if there's a need to change the plan (for example, add additional volunteers or do additional training).
- After one year, the task force will evaluate the entire program and recommend whether to expand, drop, change, or leave it as is.

Do you see how the objective has been sharpened and focused into clear steps in an action plan? There's no painful detail, but enough information to let everyone make decisions that make sense—and that are based on a written plan.

Why You Need to Stay Flexible

Action plans can be very fluid. Small wonder, considering how quickly circumstances can change!

Once a volunteer is in place, be open to changing your action plans. Agree up front that you'll change anything that you both agree to and that you'll always do so in writing. This is good practice if you only have a few volunteers; it's *essential* if you have a large number of volunteers. Putting things in writing builds trust because both you and your volunteers know you're on the same page.

> "All of these steps build on each other."

Remember that all of these steps build on each other up to this point.

If your vision changes, your mission statement will need to be reworked. If that happens, you need to revisit your goals and sharpen them into solid objectives. If you change objectives, you need to revise your action plan. It's like a line of dominoes; if the first one falls, the rest will be impacted, too.

While this sounds like it could be a lot of work, don't be discouraged. Chances are if things change quickly, it means you're headed in good directions. If other changes happen—for example, you set an objective to recruit three adult Sunday school teachers before fall classes start, and your new volunteers quit before they finish their assignment—you need to revise your plans to reflect how you'll retain future volunteers.

And please don't view changing plans as failure. That's very often not the case. Plans change when you work with people—especially when you work with people in a ministry setting where you need to be sensitive to

God's leading and to the people with whom you're working. That's part of the landscape. Flexibility isn't a luxury—it's a necessity.

Consider the Apostle Paul. His epistles are peppered with references like this passage written to the church in Rome:

> *I do not want you to be unaware, brothers, that I planned many times to come to you (but have been prevented from doing so until now) in order that I might have a harvest among you, just as I have had among the other Gentiles.* (Romans 1:13)

Paul was an apostle. You'd think if *anyone* could do long-range planning with some insight, it would be Paul. But time and time again we see him changing plans, rolling with circumstances that appear, and pursuing opportunities that present themselves.

Stay flexible. It allows you to stay faithful.

We haven't covered all the steps yet in the Volunteer Equipping Planning Loop, but we'll share all ten steps with you on the next page. You'll be able to see how the steps flow, and it's a linear process.

Stay flexible. It allows you to stay faithful.

We should point out that for existing volunteer positions the process is easier because as you loop through the planning—evaluation—planning process you may not need to make any changes at all.

The Volunteer Equipping Planning Loop

1. What's your *vision?* (Refer to your vision statement.)
2. What's your *mission?* (Refer to your mission statement.)
3. What are the major *goals and objectives* that will help you fulfill your mission and support your vision?
4. What's your *action plan* for each objective?
5. Write a *position description* for the key person you'll need to recruit to complete the action plan.
6. Decide where and how you can *recruit* appropriate people to take on these jobs based on the skills and time commitment required. Remember: The abilities, skills, and passions of the volunteers must align with what the positions require.
7. Craft a *message* to communicate as you invite people to serve.
8. What *training and orientation* will volunteers need based on their experience and the requirements of the position? How will you provide the training?
9. What *supervision* will the volunteers require? (This step includes evaluating your own or the ministry leader's leadership style, as well as the supervisory style the volunteer needs.)
10. How will you recognize and evaluate your volunteers? (Keep in mind it's recognition and evaluation that keep volunteers energized!)

Notice how step 10—recognizing and evaluating volunteers—is the primary way you keep volunteers on board, motivated, and effective. This planning process is a loop; you're never finished looking ahead. And this process recognizes that the best way to retain volunteers is to do an excellent job delivering on the fundamentals such as planning, creating job descriptions, and communicating.

Here's a secret: *Volunteer retention isn't something you do as a separate campaign*. It's the logical outcome of doing other things correctly, including recognizing and evaluating volunteers. Note also that action plans (step 4) play a key role in the process. Until you've written action plans, you can't craft position descriptions or find appropriate volunteers. Action plans are *essential*.

We'll talk about position descriptions later in this book, but until you have action plans, you're not ready to write them. You don't know what you're trying to accomplish, so you don't know who you might need to get the job done.

Here's another secret for action plan success: *Don't treat all volunteers the same*. This is going to feel awkward, so promise to hear this through...

> Don't treat all volunteers the same.

If you want to see your action plans actually get implemented, make the volunteers who are responsible for shaping and carrying out those action plans your top ministry priority. If they phone, take the call. If they want to meet for coffee, get with them this week instead of next. If they e-mail, reply within 24 hours.

Wait a minute, are you protesting? You want to treat everyone fairly, so *all* your volunteers are a top priority!

If you're leading five volunteers, that's probably possible. But as your ministry grows and you're looking at a list of ten, twenty, or a hundred volunteers, they can't all be your top priority. It's physically impossible.

What do you do?

I'd suggest you decide to not treat every volunteer the same.

While you're available to any volunteer who truly needs to see you, intentionally work through those volunteers who are responsible for overseeing other volunteers. If you've placed Tricia in charge of the nursery and she has fifteen volunteers reporting to her, *work through Tricia*.

Pour your time and energy into Tricia, and let her handle issues that arise with those fifteen nursery volunteers.

You're not being mean or arrogant. You're being wise. After all, Jesus himself directed the majority of his teaching to a handful of disciples, then let them spread the word from there. Jesus was available to interact with the lepers, the ill, and the crowds of people who flocked to see him, but at the end of the day when he was providing mentoring, he sat with just a small group of disciples.

We sometimes refer to top volunteers—the people to whom we delegate significant responsibility and authority—as "achievers." They *love* achieving goals. They *love* achieving success. They do their jobs well, and they're creative, energetic, and action-oriented. They want to get moving and stay moving.

"Every construction site needs a bulldozer or two now and then."

If you don't make achievers your top priority, they may very well move on without you, and perhaps head off in the wrong direction. Or they may simply lose motivation and momentum.

If achievers find you unavailable (and *they'll* define what that term means, by the way) too often, they'll switch to another ministry assignment or even another church to find a new assignment. Treat these people well! Don't hold them back. Keep their motivation high and creativity going by never becoming an obstacle on their sprint toward progress.

Are there volunteer leaders in your church whom you've neglected in the past? Perhaps you've actually *resented* these people because their enthusiasm pushed you along faster than you wanted to go. How can you communicate with those sorts of achievers that you don't want to lose them? that they're your top priority?

Not every volunteer you have will be an achiever—but those who are may be your next level of leadership. You don't want to lose them.

Remember: Every construction site needs a bulldozer or two now and then.

8 Deciding Where Volunteers Can Serve

Before you sign up volunteers, you need to know where you'll use them. Which positions are best? Which are off-limits? Here are the guidelines.

The phone is ringing. The bell choir director wants eight volunteers by next Wednesday. The outreach ministry team leader needs fifteen people to do follow-up after an area evangelistic rally. But the treasurer, who's always complaining she has too much to do, doesn't want *any* volunteers.

And the pastor wonders who you can rustle up to run the annual all-church picnic. The pastor wants anyone *but* Mrs. Eresman, who unexpectedly substituted soy burgers for the hamburgers last year because she's a vegetarian.

Or maybe the phone *isn't* ringing. Other than in Sunday school and vacation Bible school, there's no place volunteers are welcome to serve in your church. The other jobs are done by paid staff who have made it clear: Off Limits to Volunteers. So as you recruit people with great abilities and skills, people who want to serve in areas of ministry they're passionate about, there's no room for them. They aren't welcome.

What do you do? Where do you place volunteers?

Three Guidelines for Placing Volunteers

In light of the three theologies we discussed earlier—the priesthood of all believers, the giftedness of each child of God, and the whole body of Christ, we'd like to suggest these three guidelines when it comes to placing volunteers in your church.

1. Place volunteers where they're wanted.

If you place volunteers where they aren't truly wanted, the experience will be negative for everyone involved. The volunteers' expectations won't be met, adequate supervision won't be provided, and nobody will emerge a winner.

If you're in a church where volunteers haven't been used much, we suggest this: Look for ministry leaders who are willing to work with volunteers. Start there. Let your success build based on the glowing reports that come from busy staffers who now have more time, more energy, and more opportunity to expand the scope of their ministries because volunteers are shouldering some of the load.

2. Place volunteers where they want to go.

Place people in roles that match their unique, God-given abilities, skills, and passions for ministry. Dropping someone into the wrong position is a recipe for disaster.

3. Place volunteers in expanded placement opportunities.

Okay, you've never had a volunteer do premarital counseling. But could a volunteer handle that role? Absolutely. There's not a job at your church that a volunteer can't potentially fill, even if the role requires ordination. Many churches have retired clergy who are ready and available to step in if needed and are serving in this capacity.

> "There are no limitations on where God can use volunteers in your church."

From filling the pulpit to filing the tax forms, there are often people who have the ability to make meaningful contributions. God has given them the requisite gifts; it's up to your church to provide the requisite opportunities.

The bottom line: *There are no limitations on where God can use* volunteers *in your church.*

The only obstacles are the willingness of your leadership to use volunteers and the abilities, skills, and passions of the volunteers themselves.

So we're really asking the wrong question if we ask "Where can we place volunteers?"

The questions we *should* be asking are:

- *Is there truly a need for a volunteer ministry at our church?* (The answer is "yes," by the way, for all the reasons explained earlier.)
- *Is that need felt by the church leadership?* (This may be true of some ministry area leaders and not others.)
- *Where are the places that ministry need and volunteer abilities, skills, and passions overlap?* (To get this information you'll need to interview both the ministry leaders and volunteers—there's no shortcut on this process.)

Some leaders of ministry areas like children's church and youth ministry have a long history of incorporating volunteers. Even the curriculum available for some ministry areas assumes that volunteers will be leading the programs, and it is written accordingly.

Other areas of ministry have less history—or none at all. Often the pastoral aspects of ministry are delivered by paid staff only. True, performing marriage ceremonies is a matter of licensing; not just anyone can do it. But premarital counseling can be done by volunteers, and so can other types of counseling and emotional care. Sermons can be delivered by volunteers, too.

You can't force a ministry leader to take on volunteers; you need the leader's support and enthusiasm for the volunteer placement to thrive.

But you *can* look for ministry leaders who are clearly too busy. They're ripe for a discussion about what volunteers can—and can't—do for them.

No matter what a leader is willing to do to accommodate volunteers, if the leader won't do *this*—run away. Don't place a volunteer with that leader.

Approaching the Maxed-Out Ministry Leader

I've met many people—in corporations, nonprofit agencies, and churches—who feel overworked, understaffed, and underfunded. Of course, in many churches, those feelings are completely justified. They *are* overworked... understaffed...*and* underfunded!

Especially when the economy takes a turn for the worse, churches have to watch the purse strings. Although a church may not technically "lay off" a staff member, sometimes open positions aren't filled and the remaining staff is spread thinner.

Other times, a staff member may see the need to expand the ministry, and he or she deeply desires to add a bus route, open a food pantry, or make sure each visitor gets a personal phone call as a follow-up gesture.

But without more people, those dreams go unrealized.

> "Perhaps that's where some of your ministry leaders are now—stretched thin and maxed out."

Perhaps that's where some of your ministry leaders are now—stretched thin and maxed out. They feel too busy, as if they're rowing as fast as they can but still they can't make headway upstream. They need more hands and more feet.

If you're directing a ministry area in your church, perhaps *you* feel that way about your corner of the world. You're frustrated. You need more volunteers. And you're *willing* to work with qualified volunteers. Bring them on!

And that may be the biggest hurdle for a maxed-out ministry leader. That leader has to pause long enough to actually train a volunteer. And nothing sounds less appealing to someone frantically stamping out a grass fire than to stop stamping long enough to explain to someone *else* how to stamp out fires.

So recognize that not every ministry leader in your church may be ready to use volunteers. That's okay—place volunteers in the soil where they'll be welcome and where they'll bloom. Start with the ministry areas where the leaders *are* ready and the volunteers will thrive.

> Not every ministry leader in your church may be ready to use volunteers.

Don't miss that point: *Place volunteers only where they're wanted and valued.* If a leader doesn't want volunteers, don't force the issue. It's the volunteers who will pay for your insistence.

And as you talk with leaders who show an enthusiasm for using volunteers, I urge you to gently test their true readiness by working through the following questionnaire with them.

Ministry Leader Questionnaire

- Do you believe in the priesthood of believers in 1 Peter 2:9?
- Do you truly believe that all Christians are called to be active in ministry?
- Do you believe that God gives each of his children a unique set of abilities, skills, and passions—a giftedness—to use for serving others and to glorify God?

  (Okay, maybe you can agree with those questions—they're biblical and it's pretty easy to nod your head to them in theory. But let's bring it down another level.)
- Do you believe that because of their giftedness, the people in your church have something valuable to contribute?
- Are you willing to help people in your church learn where to use their abilities, skills, and passions?

(continued on next page)

- Are you willing to examine your own areas of responsibility so that you'll begin to use volunteers to do ministry alongside you?

  (The questions keep getting harder, don't they? We're not finished yet. If you're truly serious about working effectively with volunteers, then you finally need to ask yourself these questions.)

- Do you have enough confidence in *yourself* to not only accept, but actually to look for people who know more about something than you do in an area where you need help?
- Are you willing to delegate major parts of your ministry to gifted and qualified volunteers—and be thrilled, not threatened, when they succeed?
- Are you willing to offer positions that match the volunteers you find, including ones with a high level of involvement—jobs that make sense as a logical "whole" and fulfilling position, that go beyond busywork, and that truly offer volunteers the opportunity for satisfaction and growth?
- Are you willing to move from being a "doer" of everything to being an "equipper"?

You can feel comfortable asking leaders these kinds of questions because you'll have to ask *yourself* the same questions many times.

We're guessing that you as a leader also occasionally trip up because of your own blind spots. You think you can do it all or that only you can do it right. Sound familiar? That's because you're human, just like everyone else.

So pause now and read through the Ministry Leader Questionnaire again—this time with a pencil in your hand. Answer these questions for and about yourself.

Or—if you're *really* brave—go through them with someone you trust who knows your work style and values. Make notes about your attitudes. Start thinking of tasks within the volunteer ministry of which you're protective and that you might need to delegate to a volunteer. Do any people in your church come to mind who might step in to help you in those areas?

Remember: You've got to walk the talk. You've got to model the behavior you want to see in other leaders. If *you* won't trust volunteers to do significant ministry, why would you expect other leaders to do so?

> If you won't trust volunteers to do significant ministry, why would you expect other leaders to do so?

And there's another reason for you to make the volunteer ministry the poster child for how volunteers can be effective: It will help you know what other ministry leaders think and feel. You've worked so hard on this volunteer initiative—are you really going to turn it over to a bunch of...*volunteers?*

Yes. And because you do, that means the children's pastor who has labored to create a vacation Bible school that pulls in kids from all over town can entrust that effort to a volunteer. And the pastor can trust a volunteer to visit a church member in the hospital. And the youth director can trust a volunteer to pull together the fall retreat.

Placing volunteers doesn't happen in a vacuum. Each of those volunteers is placed in a ministry and will most likely report to and be supervised by someone. You go a long way toward helping volunteers succeed by making certain those leaders and supervisors are ready and prepared to work with the volunteers in their ministry areas.

And two things you can do to assure a successful placement are to help leaders work through creating position descriptions and to learn to delegate well.

Let's start with position descriptions.

9

Designing Ministry Descriptions That Work

What? Job descriptions in the church? You bet—and here's why this step in the volunteer placement process is worth its weight in gold. Plus you'll get step-by-step help in creating crisp, clear position descriptions.

Have you seen the TV show where they do a home make-over? The premise of the show is that a team goes into someone's home and in just a few days completely redecorates a room or two—or even the whole house.

Anyway, when you're watching the team of remodelers get started, it's frantic activity. They've got a limited amount of time, so they're hurrying along as fast as they can. Maybe they already knew what they planned to do, or perhaps they're just wired to plunge right into projects. And of course, they want the best for their friend or family member—the person in whose home they're working.

But once in a while, you'll catch a glimpse of someone in the background who's just standing around, looking lost. This person probably has some skills or he wouldn't be there. And his passion for getting the job done is just as high as the others who are helping—he wants his homeowner-friend to be pleased when the surprise is revealed. So why is this person standing in the midst of the chaos, surrounded by others panicked that they might not finish on time, yet appearing to have nothing to do?

Probably because no one has said, "You're good at sewing? Here, make these new draperies." Or "You know how to use power tools and read a plan? Here, build a desk for the den."

People in churches are a lot like the people on that television show. Some—the ones that seem to be doing everything—are what we call the "Pillars" of the church. Other people who don't seem to be doing anything we refer to as the "Pewsitters." The Pewsitters *always* outnumber the Pillars.

Unfortunately, the Pillars in most churches are burning out (maybe you've been one in the past and you've changed churches or "gone underground" for a while to get a break). Meanwhile, the Pewsitters wander off, feeling left out and unneeded.

It's a terrible cycle, and it totally undermines the three theologies we explored earlier. People with something to offer aren't involved. People who have one set of skills are forced into inappropriate jobs because *someone* has to do it. And one after another, the Pillars topple out of exhaustion.

The Pewsitter's Dilemma

Pastors and other church leaders like to blame the vast majority of the people in their churches—those pesky Pewsitters—for not volunteering to help with the church's overall ministry, or serve in any church programs. Of course, sometimes the reason is as simple as the fact no one has asked.

But beyond that, many Pewsitters just don't *know* what they'd do if they volunteered. They come to church week after week, and they see mostly the same people doing the visible tasks. The same people sing. The same people teach. The same people collect the offering and make the announcements.

> Many Pewsitters just don't know *what* they'd do if they volunteered.

And it can be hard for people to describe if they're being left out. It can be tough to express something that may just seem to be an indescribable feeling. They can't put into words:

- what they think they're good at,
- what they got tired of doing when they volunteered before,
- what they know they don't like to do,
- what they want to learn, or
- where they're being led to grow.

The following is an all-too-familiar occurrence at many churches...

Jack had attended First Church for a few years and had decided it was time he found a place to serve. Jack was a banker by trade, and one thing he knew was that he *didn't* want to serve in a financial role. He did that all week long.

But Jack was intrigued by the idea of teaching in the preschool department. Jack loved the years his own children were preschoolers, and he's the big-teddy-bear kind of guy preschoolers instinctively love.

So Jack filled out a survey and eagerly described his interest, his education, and his experience working with preschoolers. He even indicated a willingness to help each week in the preschool class, since he knew how important it is for preschoolers to have consistency.

About a month later, Jack still hadn't heard from anyone at church about his volunteer interests. Yet as he sat down for the worship service and opened his bulletin, he saw an announcement that shocked him. Rita—who already was the president of the women's ministry at church, helped organize the annual missions festival, and sang in the church choir—was being recognized as the new volunteer serving weekly in the church's preschool class.

Of course, probably no one meant to overlook Jack. But the message he likely received was "They just want me for my money" or "I guess they don't want men working as volunteers in Christian education."

And no one meant to overuse Rita, who's clearly a Pillar. But churches seem to burn people like Rita out and let people like Jack stay on the sidelines.

How are you doing with connecting people with ministry opportunities? Have you delegated an appropriate ministry to everyone who's willing to do something? You may think the answer is "yes," since your appeals for volunteers seem to fall on deaf ears.

> Affirm them—they deserve it!

But check your assumption using the survey on the next page. Politely talk with people as they leave your church's services. Ask, "Do you currently volunteer to help with any ministries in our church?" For those who say "yes," you can politely ask about their involvement and thank them. Affirm them—they deserve it!

But for those who say "no," ask them which of the listed choices describe why they don't volunteer.

Please *don't* use this as an opportunity to sign people up for existing volunteer openings. You'll need to interview each person and place them according to their gifts, skills, and passions to be effective.

Your goal is to find out why Pewsitters are sitting instead of plugging into church programs as volunteers. Position your survey-takers where they can interview people without creating a bottleneck or delay parents picking their children up from classrooms. And if someone doesn't want to participate, respect that.

Volunteer Survey

Ask the following question of every person that passes. Please indicate whether the person you're interviewing is a child (12 or under), a teenager (13-19), or an adult.

"Do you currently volunteer to help with any ministries in the church?"

If the answer is *yes*, politely ask about their involvement and affirm the person.

If the answer is no, ask which of the following choices describes why they don't volunteer:

____ I'm new, so I don't know where I fit in yet.

____ I've volunteered in the past, but I'm taking some time off right now.

____ I've never been asked.

____ I don't know what ministries need volunteers.

____ I've indicated that I'm available, but no one has contacted me.

____ Other: ________________________________

____ Child ____ Teenager ____ Adult

How to Get People Out of the Pews

You've discovered a lot about yourself and your ministry. Maybe you're now aware that if you had some volunteer help you could be more effective in your area of ministry. You might find people who are even more gifted than you are to accomplish some of the responsibilities in your position.

And that would let you do two things: Focus on the parts of your ministry you really enjoy, and expand the scope of your ministry as you take on new tasks—and as you delegate new responsibilities to volunteers.

And now you hear that many people in your church would volunteer if they knew what to do and knew that someone was needed to do it!

So...why don't they sign up?

Let's explore at least part of the solution to this problem. It's the next step in the process of a volunteer ministry: designing positions for volunteers to do.

Our use of the word "design" is intentional. We're not just trying to use a sophisticated term for writing job descriptions (although it's also okay to use that term). But we like to keep the word "design" in mind because it helps keep the central focus on artistically and skillfully planning positions that your volunteers will do—and enjoy doing! The more creative and detailed you can be, the more likely the volunteer who fills the position will be content—even joyful—about serving in it.

Essentially, you'll list all the work that needs to be done—the responsibilities and tasks that can be accomplished by position. Then you'll divide those responsibilities and tasks into positions that are appropriate for various volunteers.

"A well-designed position description is an invaluable tool for recruiting the right volunteers."

Take this task seriously. A well-designed position description is an invaluable tool for recruiting the right volunteers.

This tool allows you or your interviewers to do a better job of interviewing potential volunteers. A well-designed position description will help you determine if the volunteer needs any training. And it will help you evaluate the volunteer's performance and measure whether or not using volunteers in your ministry is successful.

The Importance of Designing Serving Positions

Until you can explain what a volunteer is supposed to do, most potential volunteers won't agree to come on board to give you a hand. Nor should they—because you aren't ready to put them to work doing something significant.

Unfortunately, when you have 47 kids running around at your youth group meeting or a bursting-at-the-seams Sunday school, it's tempting to recruit volunteers just to gain some manpower. But if they don't know what to do—what you expect of them or how they can make a difference with the people they're serving—you'll quickly lose many of those volunteers.

Recruiting volunteers before you design positions is like trying to dance before the music starts. Sure, you can start dancing, but there's a good chance that you'll end up out of step once the music begins.

> "Recruiting volunteers before you design positions is like trying to dance before the music starts."

When Marlene Wilson left the corporate world and started leading volunteers in nonprofit organizations, she interviewed dozens of volunteers who were leaving agencies.

When asked why they'd quit, they often answered, "I was never really clear on what I was supposed to do, and I didn't even know who to ask for help."

Agencies had been driven by their need to fill a certain number of volunteer slots. They thought they could simply get people into place and then figure out what to do. Most often, that didn't work well.

It *still* doesn't work well. Not at agencies, and not at your church.

What Volunteers Want—and Need

Some church leaders feel it's too business-like to have position descriptions for volunteer roles. They seem to think that getting organized by designing roles for volunteers is somehow not trusting God. But without position descriptions volunteers are miserable. They're ineffective. They're unsure they're doing the right stuff.

When you make sure people's abilities, skills, and passions match the volunteer position, you demonstrate that you care more about your volunteers than your own need to fill jobs. You show you're not willing to toss volunteers into roles and then watch to see whether they sink or swim.

This might not seem overly important to some leaders in churches. But think how many people get hurt, and even leave the church, because of wounds they receive while volunteering in the wrong place. They fill a position, but they aren't recognized for it. They may even be criticized because they're failing at a task that wasn't an appropriate fit for them in the first place.

Volunteers want the benefits that come from having position descriptions. They need the clarity and the knowledge that the position they're signing up to handle has been thought through and defined.

"Volunteers want the benefits that come from having position descriptions."

Position descriptions can help you be sure that you're providing consistent service in your church or ministry. They help you evaluate whether volunteers are meeting the standards and providing the quality the position requires. They demonstrate to volunteers that you take what they do seriously and that you don't see them as frivolous contributors to your church or ministry. They help your volunteers understand exactly what you expect from them—what you'll hold them accountable for.

When you put ministry descriptions in place, your volunteers know that you value them, that you trust them, and that they're making a difference in the lives of the people your church or area of ministry serves.

Designing Positions That Fit Both You and Your Volunteers

So, as you start to design positions, realize that this process is part of the total culture of what you're doing with volunteers within your ministry or as a whole within your church.

Take your leadership style, for example. If you're a rather loose manager of people, you can't design positions that require constant and close supervision. If you do, both you and your volunteers will fail. You might recruit the right kind of person, someone who needs a lot of supervision. Yet your style won't provide enough encouragement, correction, and feedback, and the volunteer will probably feel lost.

Or, if you could be described as rather controlling and autocratic in your leadership style, don't design positions or recruit people who are creative or achievement-oriented. You'll only hold them back, and again, both you and the volunteers will be frustrated.

It's fairly easy to keep your leadership style in mind when you're designing positions for volunteers who report to you, but what about a position that reports to another person? What do you do then? Does it makes sense to build in that consideration for volunteers who report to the head custodian, a job that seems to be filled by a different person every six months?

Do this: Make certain you cover supervisors' leadership styles in the interview process. If it's a significant factor, deal with it in the position description. Typically that's not the case, and the issue can be explored in the context of an interview.

Levels of Involvement

When you create position descriptions for volunteers in your church or area of ministry, you're going to discover that some volunteers want very light involvement. Other volunteers desire intense involvement, and still others are looking for every level in between.

To help everyone find a way to contribute and to successfully recruit the right volunteers to fill the right positions, you'll need to come up with several levels of involvement for various jobs or tasks. For example, if you run a food pantry as part of your ministry, you might have job responsibilities that include:

Lightest involvement: Donate money or food to food pantry.

Moderate involvement: Work in food distribution center sorting donated items and assembling grocery bags.

Heavier involvement: Coordinate the work of volunteers to deliver food to needy families in the community. (See also page 173, "Sample Position Descriptions.")

Creating several levels of involvement allows volunteers to find positions that match their skills, desires, and the level of commitment they can offer. Due to time limitations, family responsibilities, or just a desire to serve in a helping role, some volunteers want to do routine or sporadic tasks.

But volunteers who wish to commit more time and who have the appropriate skills may be looking for more. Also, some volunteers who start at the lightest level of commitment may want to move to a higher level of commitment after testing the waters. Knowing they have this option can be comforting and motivating.

> It's wise to stay flexible in the types of positions you offer and how you define those roles.

It's wise to stay flexible in the types of positions you offer and how you define those roles.

Some volunteers are willing to assume very responsible assignments, and for those sorts of positions we urge you to design "volunteer professional" level positions.

A "volunteer professional" position is one that defines the broad areas of responsibility but doesn't spell out every specific task required to fulfill these responsibilities. It also won't specify the time and manpower needed, because it's up to the volunteer to decide how to best fulfill the responsibility. The volunteer selects his or her own staff from the potential volunteers who have been interviewed.

Often, the less responsible the position, the more specific you need to be with your descriptions. The volunteers who consider these positions need to know exactly what you expect of them in terms of time requirements, duties, and details. Also, be clear about what skills are required. These detailed descriptions help volunteers determine if the job fits the realities of their lives.

Remember: If a volunteer has a good experience at a less-demanding level, he or she might take an interest in assuming more responsibility.

When determining levels of responsibility, it helps if you imagine an inverted pyramid.

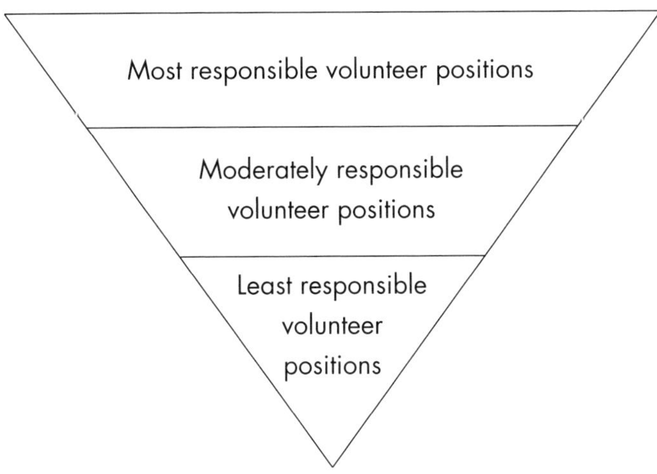

Most responsible volunteer positions (for example, design Sunday worship experiences)

- Define broad areas of responsibility and authority.
- Assign responsibility rather than specific and detailed tasks.
- Allow volunteer to determine and negotiate needs.
- Define skills and abilities required for the position.
- Leave room for initiative and creativity in how responsibility is carried out.

Moderately responsible volunteer positions (for example, create skit to illustrate sermon)

- Spell out tasks fairly well.
- List time requirements and define levels of skill required.
- Indicate lines of responsibility and authority.

Least responsible volunteer positions (for example, pass offering plates)

- Clearly define duties, time, and skills required.
- List specific tasks.
- Spell out exactly what needs to be done and when.

Discovering What Motivates People

One other thing to keep in mind about designing positions for volunteers is that the descriptions need to include motivators or benefits. Do the positions allow volunteers the opportunity to develop new skills or learn something new about themselves? The worst jobs are ones that are so rigidly constructed that the volunteers feel that they either need to fit into that box or they'll just have to move on. And clarity counts; the best ministry descriptions are precise and concise, rather than elaborate or complicated.

"The best ministry descriptions are precise and concise, rather than elaborate or complicated."

When you match the motivational needs of volunteers to appropriate position descriptions, you'll see both motivation and performance improve. And don't guess what motivates people; you can know for sure if you ask them or observe them.

You can't overestimate the motivational power of lining up a position with people's goals for themselves. Why does each volunteer want to be involved in your ministry? Most volunteers will have at least two goals:

1. They want to use their abilities to grow or develop.
2. They want to answer their call to serve others.

> And don't guess what motivates people; you can know for sure if you ask them or observe them.

As you work with individual volunteers in your ministry, you'll have opportunity to help them stretch. You want them to be realistic about their abilities and involvement, but you also want them to move at least a bit out of their comfort zone. It's a balance—and one you'll need to keep for your overall ministry goals and objectives, as well.

A note: If you lead a large volunteer program, you may be able to provide this level of care only for the volunteers who report directly to you. If that's the case, model how to connect positions with motivations, and encourage these volunteer supervisors to do the same for the people who report to them.

The following worksheet can help potential volunteers learn a little more about themselves and help them understand why they're volunteering. Feel free to copy it and use in interviews or give it to volunteers for self-assessments.

Why I Volunteer

1. As I'm involved in my volunteer role, I want to achieve the following goals:

2. What are some of the positive things that might happen if I reach these goals?

3. What are my chances for success?

(Place a mark on the following line for each goal you identified

Very good——good——fair——poor——very poor

4. Why do I feel this way?

5. What are some of the negative things that might happen if I reach these goals?

____

____

____

____

6. What could keep me from reaching my goal(s)?

____ I don't really have the skills, ability, and/or knowledge needed.

____ I don't want it badly enough to really work for it.

____ I'm afraid that I might fail.

____ I'm afraid of what others might think.

____ Others don't want me to reach this goal.

____ This goal is really too difficult to ever accomplish.

____ Other reasons: ____

7. What are some things I could do so the obstacles listed above don't prevent me from reaching my goals?

____

____

____

____

8. Do I still want to try to reach these goals?

____ Yes

____ No

____ Undecided

(continued on next page)

9. Who can help me reach these goals?

Name:

___

Kind of help:

___

___

___

___

10. What are some first steps I can take to reach these goals?

___

___

___

___

11. What else do I need to do if I really want to succeed?

___

___

___

___

12. Will I take the above steps?

____ Yes

____ No

____ Undecided

13. If you answered yes to item 12, make the following self-contract. Write a self-contract for each goal you've decided to meet.

Self-Contract

I've decided to try to achieve the goal of ______________.
The first step I'll take to reach my goal is ______________.
My target date for reaching my goal is______________.

Signed:______________________________

Date:______________________________

Witnessed by: ______________________________

How You Can Make Existing Positions Better

What should you do about positions that volunteers are already filling? As long as someone is accomplishing those tasks, should you leave them alone and assume that everything is fine?

That's a dangerous assumption. Most positions can be improved if you examine them closely.

If someone is filling a volunteer position and is content in the job, you can simply match the position description to the person. But if you have positions that have been tough to fill, or that are plagued with repeated volunteer turnover, designing new descriptions will help solve those problems.

"Most positions can be improved if you examine them closely."

Ask yourself if the volunteer roles in your area of ministry are interesting and challenging enough to hold people in them. Ask your current volunteers what they think of their position descriptions and how they'd improve their ministry. Together with your current volunteers, go through your position descriptions and see if you can come up with ways to enlarge or enrich them or just make them more fun.

The following process can help you revise a position description that's not working.

How to Fix a Broken Position Description

Start with a volunteer position that's tough to fill or that has suffered from frequent turnover. Use one or more of the following techniques to make the position more appealing.

1. **Enlarge**—List additional tasks that you could include in this position.
2. **Enrich**—List functions that might be more managerial that a volunteer could take over.
3. **Simplify**—List tasks that have turned out to be menial and remove them from the position, or combine tasks that could be done more easily by one volunteer.
4. **Add variety**—Add tasks that spice up a position to make dull or routine tasks more appealing.
5. **Create continuity**—Add steps that make a job feel more whole; this can add appeal to a position that requires a single task to be done over and over.

Nuts and Bolts of Writing Ministry Descriptions

Let's assume the worst: You've inherited a volunteer ministry that has dozens of volunteers already serving (that's good!) and you're in need of another dozen volunteers (that's less good) and you have exactly zero position descriptions on file. All the current volunteers were recruited with verbal descriptions of what they'd do, and for the most part they've adapted.

The volunteers you still need are waiting to hear what you want them to do, and position descriptions would certainly help. So you need to work in two directions: Create position descriptions for the people who are already serving, and create them for the positions you need to fill so you can place the right people in those positions.

Don't worry—creating ministry descriptions isn't really all that complicated. It requires focus and information, but you can develop the first and gather the second. And as you'll see from the sample position description outline below, you don't have to worry about the format of the forms. You can create an outline, use bullet points, or simply write descriptions in paragraph form. Nobody is going to grade you on format or font selection.

"Creating ministry descriptions isn't really all that complicated."

Just make certain that each position description clearly contains the following:

- Position title
- Goal of the position
- Who the volunteer is responsible to or reports to
- A two or three sentence summary (or list of points) describing the tasks
- The approximate time required per week or month
- The "term" of the commitment, stated in days, months, or years
- A description of the training that will be provided
- A list of any special qualifications or unique skills the position requires
- The benefits that the volunteer will receive for doing and completing the position.

Use these items as a checklist to be sure position descriptions you write include all the relevant information. Again, writing style and format matter far less than clarity!

Gathering Information

If you're working on a position description for a person that will report to you, gathering the necessary information is no problem. You know who the volunteer will report to and what the volunteer is expected to do.

But what if you're in a huge church where you aren't even certain what some volunteers do? What if the volunteer will serve as the associate choirmaster? You may have exactly zero idea of what an associate choirmaster does and might be uncertain if the volunteer will report to the choirmaster, the choir director, or the choir coordinator.

> Sit down with the person who will be supervising the volunteer and help *that* person write the position description.

How can you write a position description when you're in the dark about details? The short answer is: You can't. Instead, you need to sit down with the person who will be supervising the volunteer and help *that* person write the position description.

That's why it's so important that you become comfortable creating ministry descriptions; the odds are good that you'll be coaching others on how to do it. We suggest this quick process for getting busy ministry area leaders to stop and focus on creating solid position descriptions.

- **Refuse to place volunteers until position descriptions are complete.**

  It's important that ministry leaders understand that position descriptions aren't just paperwork. They're essential for the placement process—and you can't work without them. Stand firm on your need for both the written position description and the clarity and thought that went into crafting it. You're being an advocate for the success of your volunteers and the volunteer ministry if you insist on volunteer supervisors having a clear understanding of what—and who—they need.

- **Give volunteer supervisors the checklist you used to create your own position description.**

  You're delegating the responsibility to create position descriptions. That means you've got to provide all the information necessary to complete the job.

- **Give volunteer supervisors sample position descriptions.**

  Use those we've provided or samples from your church. The task of creating descriptions is less intimidating when you've got a short stack of samples to use as models.

- **Review position descriptions with the ministry leaders who create them.**

  This brief meeting allows you to clear up any uncertainty you may have about what was written and make sure the job descriptions reflect what's really desired. Plus, you'll be able to thank and affirm the leaders who take time to create position descriptions.

> Thank and affirm the leaders who take time to create job descriptions.

- **Revisit position descriptions after volunteers have been placed.**

  Six weeks to six months after a volunteer is actually doing the job, it's a good idea to talk with both the volunteer and the volunteer's supervisor. Is the volunteer actually doing what was anticipated when the position description was written? If not, make adjustments to reflect reality.

Clear, crisp position descriptions go a long way toward getting the right people in the right spots—and making volunteering fulfilling and a boost to spiritual growth.

But another piece of the puzzle is equally important and something the volunteer really can't control. It's the willingness of a volunteer's supervisor to *delegate*. Without the ability to delegate, ministry leaders don't allow volunteers to do anything significant.

Until your ministry leaders master the skill of delegation, your volunteers won't find their ministry experiences as rich as expected, and ministry leaders will struggle with managing volunteers.

Let's deal with delegation next—before you place the volunteers in the care of supervisors who aren't sure how to make the best use of their willingness to serve!

10

Delegation

Before you place a volunteer, make sure a ministry leader is ready to give that volunteer a significant role. These fundamentals of delegation will help your ministry leaders—and you—work well with volunteers.

Delegation is the process of identifying a responsibility and transferring it, and the authority to meet it, to another person. It's thinking through—ahead of time—how to share work.

And that seems so simple—until you try to actually *do* it.

The problem is that it's one thing to assign a responsibility to another person. It's another thing to also transfer the power required to accomplish that responsibility. Most of us are good at giving away the job, but not so good at giving away the power to do it.

When the responsibility and necessary power travel together, that's delegation. When the responsibility is given without the power to do it, that's not delegation. It's dumping. Here's an example of the difference…

Suppose Jack is a volunteer in the youth department. The youth pastor approaches Jack and explains that there's a youth group lock-in on the calendar in two months. The pastor wants Jack to plan the program and run with it.

Jack asks questions about budget, schedule, and programming. The youth pastor has already gathered all that information, and he passes the file over with a warm "thank you" and a promise to check in weekly to keep up with progress. The youth pastor tells Jack to pull together the program and recruit helpers; he's got the authority to call any youth volunteer who's been background screened and cleared and ask that person to help.

Jack has been delegated a task, and he's excited about making the next lock-in both fun and spiritually significant. He understands the goals and has the information he needs to get started. Plus, he's got a weekly "touch base" to get questions answered.

That's delegation.

Now suppose instead that the youth pastor catches Jack in the hallway after church Sunday morning and explains that nothing has been done about the youth group lock-in that's scheduled next Friday. The youth pastor had intended to get things started earlier, but other commitments kept getting in the way. The youth pastor begs Jack to take on the project, and after some arm-twisting, Jack agrees.

It's not until after the youth pastor says, "Thanks for saving me, Jack!" and slips away that Jack realizes he doesn't really understand what the point of a lock-in is. He doesn't know how much money he has to spend, or how to go about organizing the event. He's not sure where he'll be able to get information or help.

That's *not* delegation—it's dumping.

> There's way too much dumping when it comes to volunteers.

There's way too much dumping when it comes to volunteers.

If Jack survives his first lock-in, do you think he'll be back? He will if the task was delegated to him, but if it was dumped on him, he'd be crazy to ever take another assignment. And the message the youth pastor just communicated said that he was the minister and Jack was "just a volunteer." He didn't help Jack understand his calling to the priesthood of believers.

Delegation will make or break your volunteer ministry. You must do it well—and do it wisely. Following are some things we've learned about delegation that will help you as you forge ahead...and they're helpful things to teach any leader who works with volunteers.

1. Choose appropriate people for assignments.

Interview and place paid and volunteer staff carefully. This is your chance to maximize strengths and compensate for weaknesses. Seek out skills and knowledge that each person needs to do his or her assignment successfully.

2. Define responsibilities clearly and creatively.

Each person needs to know what he or she is doing. It helps some people to think of the assignment as a framed blank canvas. You describe what the basic finished painting will look like, and that you expect it to fit on the canvas and within the frame you've provided. But the colors, the brush marks, and the decision about who helps finish the painting are up to the artist. This can help the person you're delegating to know where he or she can function freely, and where there are limits.

3. Delegate segments of a job that make sense.

Some positions can be divided more than others; don't assign bits and pieces of a role that won't feel significant to the volunteer. You might function best by delegating a whole area of your ministry to a volunteer. That person then recruits other volunteers to work under him or her. Make sure that those people report to your volunteer leader rather than to you. You want simply to hold the leader accountable for a whole segment, rather than multiple people accountable for bits and pieces of that area.

4. Set goals and standards of performance mutually.

As you develop performance standards be sure to get the buy-in of the people who'll actually supervise the ministry area in which the volunteer works. Does the Music Minister care if choir rehearsals start on time? If so, have that reflected in the choir director's position description. And when it's time to place someone in the choir director role, be sure the expectation is clear.

5. **Agree on deadlines and ways the volunteer can report progress or problems.**

Nothing stalls progress faster than a volunteer being unable to work out problems promptly. Also, reports build momentum for volunteers when they can communicate progress being made, and reporting lets ministry supervisors encourage or correct volunteers.

6. **Give accurate and honest feedback.**

People want to know how they're doing. They deserve to know. When you delegate, tell people you'll be evaluating their performance and then do so. Communicate that your intent isn't to catch them doing something wrong, but to encourage them to take appropriate risks and even make honest mistakes.

7. **Share knowledge, information, and plans.**

While you want to allow room for growth, don't let avoidable errors happen simply because others don't have information you could easily share. Let people know you'll be doing this—and how you'll be doing it.

8. **Provide necessary orientation, training, and recognition to the volunteers who report to you.**

This is the frame part of the blank canvas. Make sure volunteers know their boundaries, but then free them to work within those boundaries by arming them with the tools they need. Look over their shoulders once in a while and say "good job." Talk up their good efforts and accomplishments in front of others.

9. **Give volunteers who are capable of accomplishing significant portions of the ministry a voice in the decision making.**

Remember, they may know more about that area of your program than you do.

10. Truly delegate.

Most people, when they receive responsibility for a project, don't want you checking up on every step or taking back part of the assignment before they've had a chance to do it. Learn to let go.

By the way, as you think about delegating, you'll inevitably begin thinking of people who might be great at assuming some of *your* tasks. When you make an effort to find volunteers who know more about a topic or an area than you do—it makes you look better! If they do a great job implementing a more efficient process or effective ministry area, you look like a genius because you put them in charge and supported their efforts.

"Never be afraid of delegating to sharp people."

Never be afraid of delegating to sharp people.

What You Should Delegate

One reason many leaders have trouble delegating is that they simply don't know what they should let go of. If you're the leader of a ministry area in your church, the questions on the following page will help you determine what you can delegate when you find the right person.

This is one of those rare moments when you have a perfect excuse to spend an afternoon alone in a coffee shop or sitting under a tree in the park. You need time to think, with no interruptions. If that appeals to you and you do your best thinking in that sort of setting, go find that park bench.

Another approach is to jot down the specific tasks you do in your ministry for a few weeks. Use that log to give you the information you need to fill out the worksheet.

If you're not a church leader who'll be delegating jobs to volunteers, by all means have those leaders who will be keep a log of what they do. That will give you the information you need to create volunteer positions that report to those leaders. Or have *those* folks go sit under a tree for half a day as they work through the following worksheet.

And no, they won't *have* a half day to do this. But remind them that a half day invested now will pay huge dividends down the road, and if they're feeling over-busy and burned out, this is the first step to their getting help.

Delegation Worksheet

1. What functions—the major pieces or elements of your job—are you responsible for?
2. From this list, what is it essential that you do personally? Put an asterisk next to each of those items.
3. What other things would you like to get done or see done but haven't managed to get to yet?
4. From this list, which of these would you like to do yourself if you had the time? Put an asterisk next to each of those items.
5. Which of the remaining items from these two lists would you be willing to delegate if you could find the right person? Are any of them similar enough to each other that they could be combined into a larger job—something that could be delegated as a whole to give you more relief, as well as provide a volunteer with a meaningful role? What might those position titles be?
6. Considering those position titles, what would the ideal person for each of these jobs look like? What skills, experience, aptitudes, and spiritual maturity would he or she have?

Levels of Delegation

Question 5 in the worksheet suggests that you think about how you could combine similar responsibilities to create a larger volunteer position. One advantage of this arrangement is that the volunteer you recruit for the larger job can then recruit others to help fulfill that job. Those volunteers then report to the volunteer leader rather than directly to you. Only the volunteer leader reports to you.

Think of it this way: If it takes ten people to lead small groups in your church, would you rather have all ten of them call you to report how the weekly meetings went or prefer to call someone you recruit to run that ministry? Wouldn't it be handy to have a small group team leader?

You'll probably opt for a weekly call from your small-group team leader. If that volunteer is trained and capable, your ten small-group leaders will get great encouragement and support—and you'll get one call instead of ten.

A system that has volunteers leading volunteers requires you to train not just volunteers, but volunteer *supervisors*. If you want to have people in those roles, create position descriptions for those spots. You must be intentional about creating those positions.

Check out the Examples of Position Descriptions With Different Levels of Involvement on pages 176 and 177.

The Cost of Delegation

For ministry leaders, delegation can feel costly. It requires doing the preparation so a meaningful responsibility can be passed along. It demands thought and planning.

> "For ministry leaders, delegation can feel costly."

And, frankly, it requires giving up some power. We don't do that easily or comfortably. What happens if you hand over a job to someone who fails to do it—or do it well? How will that reflect on you? How will you relate to the person who let you down?

The call to delegate raises some questions in the minds of leaders—including you. How would you answer these?

Can you value administration as well as doing the work yourself? Some leaders find their personal value and worth in being able to do things well. Some fear that if they delegate certain areas of their ministry or program, people might not think they're doing their job.

Will your job be as fun if you just do administration? Many church leaders went into professional ministry because they enjoy the activities associated with the role. Some tasks are fun, and giving them away to volunteers will make the job far less rewarding and enjoyable.

Will things get done right? In the church it's important that things get done properly. After all, if the new members class is boring, families might choose to leave the church before they form enough relationships to be grafted into the congregation. But is it true that you're the only person who could do an adequate job in that class?

Can you share power? This is the bottom line for many leaders, because delegating is more than assigning a task; it's assigning a responsibility, with sufficient authority to fulfill that responsibility. If you want to delegate well, you must delegate the authority or empowerment that allows someone to do a meaningful job. How do you feel about that?

Good delegation involves trust. It's a two-way street: The volunteer must trust that sufficient information and power has been transferred. Otherwise the volunteer role will be difficult and will probably end in failure—and nobody likes being set up to fail.

> "Most volunteers want to do their best."

The ministry leader must trust the volunteer to fulfill the responsibility with excellence as it was described in the job description. Otherwise the people depending on the responsibility to be met will be disappointed—and the job may fall back on the ministry leader.

Here's the thing about trusting volunteers: You can generally err on the side of trusting too much. Most volunteers want to do their best, and they'll rise to meet your expectations...*if* you're clear about what those expectations are. There's another reason you want to make your position descriptions clear, concise, and achievable!

Benefits of Delegation

If the notion of delegating areas of ministry feels *odd* to you, don't worry: There are plenty of biblical examples of leaders doing precisely that.

Moses found that it was more than a full-time job just settling squabbles between people, and at his father-in-law's advice, he turned over a significant piece of his mediation responsibility to carefully chosen men.

And then there's this example of delegation described in the book of Acts:

> *In those days when the number of disciples was increasing, the Grecian Jews among them complained against the Hebraic Jews because their widows were being overlooked in the daily distribution of food. So the Twelve gathered all the disciples together and said, "It would not be right for us to neglect the ministry of the word of God in order to wait on tables. Brothers, choose seven men from among you who are known to be full of the Spirit and wisdom. We will turn this responsibility over to them and will give our attention to prayer and the ministry of the word."* (Acts 6:1-4)

Seven men were chosen whose qualifications matched the job description, and the responsibility became theirs. That freed the apostles to focus on doing what was most important in their ministry: prayer and preaching. Caring for widows wasn't a job that was dumped—it was delegated. And the results were predictably positive as the church grew.

The apostles realized something that perhaps is dawning on you and other ministry leaders in your church, too: You can't do it all. At least, you can't do it all *well*. It's time to delegate.

It takes some work to delegate—to adequately identify the task, create the position description, and locate the proper people who will fulfill the responsibility. But making the effort can breathe new life into your ministry because at last you'll be able to *catch* your breath.

Delegate well and you'll be surrounded by top-notch people who are there to help. You'll have time to dream of new ways your ministry can develop—and you'll have time to do something about those dreams.

And if the current pace of ministry is burning you out, you'll be able to lean on other people who understand and who have a stake in your being successful.

And you'll have an additional benefit: You'll personally witness God using volunteers who are growing spiritually, finding meaning, and sensing fulfillment as they live out their faith by serving others.

11

The Risk of Using Volunteers

The days of pretending bad things don't happen at church—or to the people our volunteers serve—have long since ended. How can you protect your church, your volunteers, and the people you serve?

It's a call no pastor wants to receive. Color drained from the pastor's face as he heard the news that for more than three years a volunteer in the children's ministry had been abusing children in his care.

It's a call no volunteer wants to receive. A boy in the church-sponsored midweek program claimed that the volunteer had exposed himself to the boy. Although the volunteer knew it wasn't true, a police investigation was underway.

Some risks you face in your ministry are obvious: Your building might burn down. You might have a budget crunch that takes some of your programs off-line. You might find that your attendance doubles (or triples) and suddenly your facilities must be replaced.

Because your church is growing and alive, there are risks. It comes with the territory. That's also true of your volunteer ministry.

But if one of your volunteers does something to a person he or she is serving...or if a claim is made against a volunteer you've placed in ministry...the losses are more than just a building.

Reputations crumble. Ministry is derailed. Trust is destroyed.

We're not trying to scare you, but we do want to instill a sense of urgency so you take immediate and decisive action. If you're not protecting every constituency in your ministry—the volunteers, the people they serve, and the church itself—*now* is the time to correct that oversight.

The Risks You Face

This slim book can't pretend to provide the last word in how you should proceed, but it can point you in the right direction. It will help you think through the possibilities and decide on some next steps in your process. And we'll pay extra attention to how you can protect your volunteer ministry and your volunteers.

The topic is risk management, and it needs to be on your radar screen.

Perhaps you've not thought much about risk management. But quickly answer these questions:

- Can a volunteer's acts make your church liable if another person is harmed? (The answer is yes!)
- Are your volunteers protected by law from any liability, or can your volunteers be held liable for certain actions? (The answer is that liability protection laws in most jurisdictions don't fully protect your volunteers.)
- Could your church face significant loss because of expenses incurred from a lawsuit? (Absolutely. And the financial losses are just part of the price you'd pay.)
- Are there potential volunteers who will shy away from signing up to volunteer if you're unable to describe the steps you've taken to protect them and the people they serve? (Yes. It's probably happening already.)

Why You Need to Manage Risk

Rather than dwelling on what *could* happen in the area of risk and liability, let's try to come up with some ways to manage and minimize those risks and liabilities.

The following is a pretty good definition of risk management: Risk management includes all management efforts aimed at minimizing the adverse impact that losses may have on an organization. The goal is to put in place systematic, organized processes that avoid, eliminate, or lower the chances that a loss will occur.

What's required of you to do risk management is that you identify what processes will accomplish eliminating or lowering your risks, then put those processes in place. Where risk management is concerned, talk is a great place to start, but action is required.

The consequences of not initiating risk management procedures and policies are potentially severe. Not only will your church and ministry be impacted, but individual lives of volunteers (or members of your congregation) can be tragically damaged.

> Where risk management is concerned, talk is a great place to start, but action is required.

There's a cost associated with managing risk, both in time and dollars. But as noted above, there's a cost associated with not managing risk, too.

Being found negligent just one time could result in financial damage your church or ministry couldn't survive. With the decline of "charitable immunity"—the legal doctrine that at one time protected charitable organizations from financial responsibility for causing harm—liability for most nonprofit organizations is the same as it is in for-profit businesses. So the primary goal of managing risk in your volunteer program is to create a relatively safe environment where your volunteers can carry out the mission of your church or area of ministry.

How You Can Manage Risk

Of course, you can't completely eliminate risk in your church or area of ministry. That's why we keep referring to "managing risk." Probably every volunteer and volunteer position brings some level of liability right inside your facility. Since you can't completely eliminate risks, you need to use your judgment and start by focusing on the ones that matter most.

Also, please again note that this brief chapter is just a primer on risk management. The goal is to bring this topic to your attention, to help you measure where you are in terms of risk management, and to nudge you along to get started on being proactive.

Where do you start? Take these four steps:

1. Look at each volunteer position, and identify any potential areas for liability. Again, use your judgment and concentrate on reducing risk in the areas that matter most. These will probably be areas where the people served are the most vulnerable: children and teenagers, people with disabilities, and senior adults.

2. Evaluate the ways you can manage those risks. What can you do to protect the people you serve—and your volunteers? Are you willing to proactively take steps to raise awareness and make changes?

3. Choose the means, and implement your strategy. Here's where you actually do something. Be aware that in any risk management strategy, the volunteer recruitment and placement process is thoroughly investigated. Practically speaking, that means when you're in the interview phase of volunteer recruitment you'll have to decide when to initiate background screenings of volunteers.

4. Monitor your ministries, and determine whether the means of managing the risk is meeting your church's needs and the needs of the people you're serving. Make sure the steps you've put in place are truly managing the risks you've identified.

Complete the assessment on pages 163 through 165 to gauge how well your church or your particular area of ministry currently recognizes and manages risk. The assessment looks long, but you'll cruise through it in about ten minutes.

Risk Management Assessment

Please choose one of the three answers: Yes, No, or Unsure (?). Put a check mark in the box of your choice.

General Liability and Risk Management	**Yes**	**No**	**?**
Does our church have an ongoing risk management committee?			
Have we examined the activities performed by volunteers and taken action to manage the risks?			
Do we have a policy and procedure manual for our volunteer program?			
Do we formally review the manual every year?			
Do we have general liability coverage for the volunteer program?			
Is one person responsible to review and update the liability coverage?			
Do we have events throughout the year that put us at greater risk for liability; if so, do we obtain coverage?			

Managing the Risks of Interviewing, Screening, and Terminating Volunteers	**Yes**	**No**	**?**
Do we have current position descriptions for each volunteer role in our church, including board members?			
Do volunteer position descriptions clearly indicate what qualifications are needed to fill each position?			
Do our position descriptions specify what physical requirements are required for the role?			

(continued on next page)

Managing the Risks of Interviewing, Screening, and Terminating Volunteers *(continued)*	Yes	No	?
Do we protect ourselves against discrimination in the way we write our position descriptions?			
Do we complete a background check on volunteers?			
Do we regularly review performance with volunteers and document it?			
Do we tell volunteers in their initial orientation that they'll have performance reviews? When? What will be covered?			
Do we immediately handle complaints or concerns about volunteers' behavior?			
Do we have written procedures for terminating volunteers?			
Do we provide volunteers with a written handbook regarding the policies and procedures?			
Do we clearly explain who will supervise volunteers and to whom they are responsible?			
Do we ask volunteers to sign a statement that they've received orientation and training and understand our expectations of them?			
Do volunteers understand the boundaries of their position descriptions—what they can and cannot do, where they should or should not be?			

Managing the Risk of Confidentiality	Yes	No	?
Do volunteers understand how our church defines confidentiality and privacy?			
Do volunteers understand what they can and cannot share publicly?			
Do volunteers know the consequences of breaking confidentiality?			

Managing the Risk of Personal Injury Liability	Yes	No	?
Do we explain safety procedures in working with people?			
Do we adequately post safety warnings for volunteers?			
Do we explain safety in their physical workspace?			
Do we provide general safety training for volunteers?			
Do we have an incident report process for volunteers?			
Do we require volunteers to report any incident that is not consistent with routine activities?			
Do we abide by the Right to Know Act and provide information regarding it? (Contact the U.S. Environmental Protection Agency for info.)			

Managing the Risk of Volunteer Drivers	Yes	No	?
Do we have insurance that covers volunteer drivers?			
Do we have certificates of insurance on file for volunteers driving their own vehicles?			
Are volunteers made aware that they must notify us of any changes in their insurance policy?			
Do we need or have automobile insurance above and beyond the volunteer's own coverage?			
Are volunteers made aware that they may need to notify their personal auto insurance carrier of the volunteer driving activities?			
Do we check for a current, valid driver's license?			
Do we check driving records through a Motor Vehicle Report?			
Do we provide special driving training for volunteer drivers?			

If you ended up with mostly "no" answers, a few "unsure" answers, and just a handful of "yes" answers, don't be surprised.

Many ministries and churches utterly flunk this assessment. Don't be discouraged if you see lots of room for improvement; feel motivated. The fact that you're reading this chapter and that you want to do something about risk management probably puts you ahead of most churches!

We strongly suggest that you go through this assessment with other staff members at your church. Bring it to the attention of your senior pastor and your church board. Although they might prefer to just look the other way on risk issues, having them take part in filling out the assessment will help them see how much work there is to do.

Examining Your Options

Keep in mind that there's no way you'll ever be completely free from liability unless you close the church doors and cease ministry. In our society, anyone can sue anyone at any time and for just about any reason. So even if you apply every one of the following methods and many others, you won't be completely secure. But here's a start at how you can minimize your church's liability.

- **Eliminate the risk.**

  This is pretty much what we just mentioned—closing your doors and ceasing to do ministry. But before you dismiss this idea, do some thinking. There might actually *be* some ministries in your church that you believe are too risky. There may be a program or area of ministry where volunteers serve, and it somewhat supports your mission, but you could live without it. If considerable risk is involved in that program, you might choose to eliminate that program entirely.

  For example, perhaps your church offers a free medical screening clinic to your neighborhood. Volunteer medical professionals use the church facilities and receive financial support to screen for certain health issues of low-income residents. Think about the risks. Professionals are providing the care, and they likely have malpractice insurance. But what about your church?

Could something happen in your facility that you'd be liable for? You might decide that the risk in this situation isn't worth it and eliminate the program entirely. Or if you're very committed to the ministry, you might instead financially support an off-site independent clinic to provide the same services, but with that independent organization assuming the liability in writing. A tough call—but it may be a wise one.

A tough call—but it may be a wise one.

Of course, you probably won't eliminate your youth ministry simply because it fosters relationships between adults and kids. Relationship is a key part of why your church and various ministries in the church exist at all. Instead, you'll want to have enough screening, training, and supervision in place to show that you and/or your volunteers weren't negligent in the event of a negative situation.

- **Transfer the risk.**

  This essentially means buying insurance. Or you could use some sort of contract that holds you harmless. Of course, the reality is that even with a contract, you may not be held harmless. Why? Because—as we've stated—in our society, anyone can sue anyone at any time and for just about any reason. And negligence is negligence; no contract removes your obligation to take customary precautions.

  But a signed contract, properly reviewed by legal counsel, may help reduce your liability. See pages 181 through 188 for information that one church requires from its volunteers: a covenant agreement, consent forms, reference forms, interest forms, and a signed contract.

  Is it overkill? This church doesn't think so...and neither does its lawyer. You'll need to decide for yourself.

- **Reduce the risk.**

  This means looking at ways to minimize your liabilities by having more comprehensive and up-to-date position descriptions for volunteers, policies and procedures for volunteers, supervision of volunteers, and documented training and orientation of volunteers. You can do this and tremendously decrease your risk without spending a cent. It's doing what you already do (or should be doing)—better.

  Some examples of policies that reduce risk are:

  - A volunteer driver who takes children under 18 on an activity must have another nonrelated adult along.
  - Adults can never be alone with a minor.
  - No snacks or food that include nuts or nut oils can be served.
  - All children must have signed medical release forms to participate in programs that involve travel or overnight stays.
  - Only drivers over the age of 25 can serve as volunteer drivers because 16- to 25-year-olds have a statistically greater chance of getting into accidents.

- **Retain the risk.**

  This means that your church decides to accept and retain the risk involved in the volunteer program, though you do what you can to reduce the risks. This category indicates that your board or church leadership has gone through the process of determining what risks are involved in the volunteer ministry, and your church leadership has formally decided to retain the risk. You'll want to document that your leadership reached this decision.

  The good news is that the more you're proactive about minimizing your volunteer program's risk, the less problems you'll face.

  The bad news is—again—anyone can sue anyone at any time and for just about any reason. Yet the more you document and record what you've done to be "due diligent," the harder it is to prove you were negligent.

- **Monitor and evaluate.**

  Periodically check to be sure that whatever risk management procedures and policies you've set into place are still effectively getting the job done.

Guidelines for Risk Management

The whole area of managing risks among volunteers is constantly changing. At one time, churches and other nonprofit groups had charitable immunity. But that protection has eroded. In the present, your church or ministry probably would face the same liability as any other organization or business.

Because the answer to "What should we do about risk?" continues to change, probably the best tool you can have is a set of guidelines that help you decide what's reasonable to do about risk management.

Here are some guidelines you might want to incorporate into the list you develop.

- **Recognize that the accountability we shoulder is heavier than ever.**

  Have there always been cases of abuse by staff members in positions of trust? Clearly that's the case—but now we're in a position to use technology and our policy handbooks to do a better job of preventing people who shouldn't be volunteering from being in positions where they can abuse others on our volunteer staffs. And it's not only *right* for us to take whatever steps we can to ensure safety, it's *smart.* All it takes is one lawsuit—perhaps even one allegation—to close down your ministry.

"All it takes is one lawsuit—perhaps even one allegation—to close down your ministry."

- **Acknowledge that not every volunteer position requires the same scrutiny.**

  If a volunteer will be working at home making phone calls to notify church members about an upcoming business meeting, you probably don't need to do any background checks at all. But if the volunteer's job involves making contact with others while on duty, that's a completely different situation. If those people are children, teenagers, or others who are vulnerable, use the strictest screening protocol you can practically put in place.

- **Get free advice.**

  Typically, one question raised in court is whether your church was negligent in providing background screening. Did you do what was prudent and customary? You probably don't need an Interpol screening, but if it's typical for churches and other ministries in your area to do a certain level of screening for positions, do at least as much. Talk with your peers and find out what they're doing. Share that information when others call you.

- **Expect changes.**

  Personnel screening is a dynamic field, and the rules keep changing. Investigate and re-investigate at least once per year what's happening. What's prudent and customary is driven by technology and the law; new standards appear with amazing frequency. Determine that for the benefit of your volunteers and those you serve, you will reflect excellence in this issue. If you want to do what's best for your volunteers and the people you serve, you'll stay on top of what's new and changing. Check with the experts now and then by consulting legal counsel and attending some workshops.

- **Establish a paper trail.**

  Document every screening effort. Keep information in volunteers' files, and keep files secure.

- **Be consistent.**

  Whatever you establish as your protocol, be consistent and apply it to everyone. Make no exceptions—including yourself. Have you put yourself through the screening procedure? Until you do, it's going to be difficult for you to convince others. And remember: If your church is a member of Group's Shepherd's Watch®, you qualify for discounts on background screenings. Call to find out (877-446-3247).

Benefits of Risk Management

There are many reasons to be intentional about managing risk.

There are the financial considerations: Your insurance provider may give you a discount if you have certain protocols in place. And you may avoid a devastating lawsuit.

> There arc many reasons to be intentional about managing risk.

But there's an even more important reason: Risk management protects people...including your volunteers.

Risk management is often viewed as an effort to weed out predators who might volunteer in your programs to gain access to children, teenagers, or others. And your efforts *will* help deny those people access to your church members.

Yet you're also protecting your volunteers. By adding some risk management guidelines to your training, you keep volunteers from accidentally ending up in compromising—though innocent—positions. If a teenage girl tells her adult male youth sponsor she has something private to tell him, that adult may innocently step into a room and close the door behind them so they can speak in private. When a parent rounds the corner looking for her daughter and discovers them sitting alone in a dim room behind closed doors, the assumptions aren't pretty, even if the topic of discussion was how the teenager could be more supportive of her parents.

Create a policy handbook for your volunteers. It's a good idea anyway—an *essential* idea—and it should include material that covers risk management. Be sure you include a statement about which positions require background checks. List what other screening, training, and supervision your church provides. Outline safety procedures. And include a church policy statement on confidentiality and privacy.

You can't be too proactive when it comes to risk management!

Sample Position Descriptions

The following sample position descriptions reflect different levels of commitment. They're each slightly different in format, but each spells out basic responsibilities, the essential skills a volunteer needs, and a projected time commitment.

Membership and Renewal Committee

Purpose: To integrate an evangelistic spirit into all facets of our church life: children, youth, adults, and worship. Work toward the goal of seeing more people come to know and trust Jesus Christ as Lord and Savior and commit to become members of our church. Give oversight to new member visitations, classes, and integration into our church.

Role of committee member: To ensure that all aspects of our church community reach out to our members and the greater community to invite and encourage men, women, and children to commit their lives to Jesus Christ. To encourage new believers and attenders to become committed to our church by becoming members.

Time commitment: Two-hour meeting once a month; committee serves a two- to four-month term.

Skills needed: A desire to see our church become more effective in witnessing and concern in rendering needed service that may do much to bring people to Christ and deepen the faith of the entire congregation

Benefit for the volunteer: You'll interact with people who are interested in our church and have the opportunity to share your faith.

(First Presbyterian Church, Bellevue, Washington)

Sunday School Activities Coordinator

Importance to our church: Activities that reinforce the Bible lessons and truths are exciting for children and provide them with opportunities to discover or develop creative expressions.

Responsibilities: You will plan, coordinate, and explain creative activities/crafts designed to enhance the Sunday lessons being taught. You will work with teachers, department coordinator, and resource center coordinator to make sure needed items are available. Attendance at teachers' meetings is necessary.

Time frame: Summertime is a good time for planning, and coordinating is from September to May. You need to be present during Sunday school, 9:30–10:40 a.m., every other Sunday. Teachers' meetings are held approximately once every six weeks.

Skills to be used/developed: Volunteer needs activities/crafts skills. An understanding of skill levels for different age groups will help you select appropriate activities and crafts.

Training/resources: Perusing teacher workshops, curriculum/activities displays, and Christian bookstores will provide a wealth of ideas.

Number of volunteers: We need one or more volunteers.

Benefit for the volunteer: You will have the personal satisfaction of using your creative talents in a ministry that reinforces the story of God's love for His children.

(Cross of Christ Lutheran Church, Bellevue, Washington)

Volunteerism Committee

The purpose of the volunteerism committee is to create a more effective ministry of volunteers. A Volunteer Coordinator and Assistant Volunteer Coordinator—who serve for two-year terms—will coordinate and continuously bring together volunteers with committees that have needs for volunteer service.

The volunteerism committee is divided into subcommittees to implement and share volunteerism techniques. The various duties of the committee are:

1. To prepare volunteer ministry position descriptions so every committee member has a clear expectation of what the committee will accomplish.
2. To identify volunteers in the congregation and keep a central record available for committee use.
3. To match volunteers and ministry positions while maximizing the use of all who wish to volunteer and integrating them into the mainstream of church life.
4. To orient and train volunteers.
5. To recognize volunteer service work in the congregation and in the community.
6. To help volunteers experience growth by moving from one volunteer commitment to another through evaluation.
7. To be alert to volunteerism needs and opportunities in the congregation and bring these to the attention of the Church Council and various church committees.

The Volunteer Coordinator will be the primary contact for any ministry leader who has volunteer needs in his or her area. When a person indicates an interest in the various opportunities in church volunteer ministry, the Volunteer Coordinator will put him or her in touch with the right ministry leader. The church newsletter will regularly list the Volunteer Coordinator's phone numbers.

(Our Saviour's Lutheran Church, Merrill, Wisconsin)

Examples of Position Descriptions With Different Levels of Involvement

Most Responsible Volunteer Position

Title: Volunteer Recruitment Core Team Leader (or Chairperson)

Responsible to: Director of Volunteers

Area of Responsibility: To be responsible for the recruitment of volunteers for this ministry. This includes the organization of other volunteers to assist in this effort as needed; the design of recruitment materials; and the implementation of recruitment objectives, as defined together with the Director of Volunteers and approved by the Advisory Committee.

Length of Commitment: One (1) year.

Qualifications: Organizational skills, knowledge of public relations, and ability to work well with staff and other volunteers. Knowledge of church and community is helpful.

Comments: This position carries a good deal of responsibility and thus it is recommended that it be your only (or only *major*) volunteer commitment for this year.

Moderately Responsible Volunteer Position

Title: Speakers Bureau Volunteer

Responsible to: Volunteer Recruitment Task Force Leader

Definition of Duties: Give presentations on behalf of this ministry for the purpose of recruiting more volunteers and encouraging church support of our ministry and its goals. Presentations to be given at adult Sunday school classes, small group meetings, worship services, and at other opportunities as assigned by Recruitment Task Force Leader.

Time Required: 2-4 hours per month. Generally audiences meet on Sundays, but not always.

Qualifications: Public speaking; ability to operate visual aid equipment helpful. Commitment to ministry goals and objectives and a belief in the value of volunteers. Enthusiasm is a must!

Training Provided: Orientation sessions will be arranged with staff and volunteers to thoroughly acquaint volunteer with the ministry and its needs.

Least Responsible Volunteer Position

Title: Telephone Aide

Responsible to: Volunteer Recruitment Task Force Leader and Secretary

Definition of Duties: Telephone prospective volunteers from lists obtained at speeches and presentations to set up interviews with the staff. Phoning should be done from the Office of Volunteers.

Time Required: 1 hour a week. Monday morning preferred.

Qualifications: Pleasant phone personality and ability to work congenially with staff and volunteers.

Comments: This volunteer must have transportation available, as our church office is not accessible by public transportation.

Volunteer Position Description Template

Use this template for designing job descriptions

Position title: A specific, descriptive title that neither exceeds nor diminishes the work of this position. It should give the volunteer a sense of identity, and it should define the position for other volunteers and staff. The title shouldn't distinguish whether the person is paid or unpaid; instead, it should simply reflect the work he or she will do.

Position impact: The purpose and desired outcome of this position should be tied directly to the mission and vision of the church or area of ministry. The impact statement should define how the work of this position will bring positive outcomes for those the church or area of ministry serves.

Performance standards: Responsibilities and duties should be listed as performance standards to be clear about the expectations of the person who fills the position. The list should not only include the activities or accomplishments, but the way the duties are carried out.

Qualifications: The list of qualifications should be clear and explicit. Communicate what is minimally required for this position, as well as what would be beneficial. Include education, personal characteristics, spiritual gifts, skills, abilities, and experience.

Benefits: This should describe the benefits to the volunteer in this position. State the benefits from the volunteer's perspective, not what the church or area of ministry will receive. Be sure to state benefits, not features.

Commitment required: With the people your church or ministry serves in mind, be explicit about what the requirements are for a person's commitment. How long do you expect a volunteer to serve in this position? How many hours per week, month, year? Address the issue of absenteeism.

Training: Specify the nature and length of all general and position-specific training required for this position. Be clear about what training is mandatory and what is optional.

Responsible to/responsible for: Define who the volunteer is responsible to in the church or area of ministry; define who the volunteer is responsible for if he or she serves as a volunteer leader.

Contract for Serving

Volunteer:

I, ____________________________, agree to serve in a volunteer capacity in accordance with the items listed in the position description.

Volunteer signature ____

Date ____

Ministry Leader:

I, ___________________________, agree to provide you with the information and tools to successfully accomplish the responsibilities of this position for our ministry and those we serve. I agree to support you in your efforts.

Leader signature ____

Date ____

Term of this contract:

From_______/_______/_______to ______/______/______

Action Words for Dynamic Position Descriptions

Use the following list of action words to add action to your position descriptions.

Administer
Advise
Arrange
Build
Call
Care for
Check
Communicate
Contact
Coordinate
Create
Demonstrate
Design
Encourage
Ensure
Evaluate
Experiment
Foster
Guide
Help
Improve
Initiate
Innovate
Interact
Lead
Listen
Mail
Model
Observe
Organize
Participate
Plan
Prepare
Provide
Purchase
Repair
Research
Review
Schedule
Set up
Supervise
Teach
Train
Visit
Write

Sample Forms for Volunteer Leadership

First Methodist Church Leadership Covenant

PURPOSE

To agree, as a spiritual leader of FMC, to be "above reproach" so that the world will see, hear, and respond to our leadership in directing them toward the grace of Jesus Christ, and to seek a careful, exemplary Christian lifestyle to encourage other believers and strengthen the church.

PARTICIPANTS

This agreement is for all in regular teaching positions or pastoral care positions, all staff, interns, coordinators, lay ministers, and other positions designated by pastoral leadership.

SPECIFIC AGREEMENTS

1. You have accepted Jesus Christ as your personal Savior.
2. You are a member of (or actively pursuing membership at) FMC.
3. You will work in harmony with the said policies and statement of faith of FMC.
4. You support FMC with your time, money, and loyalty, including participating in the ministries and worship services on a weekly basis.
5. You are known for a dedicated Christian life, according to the standards of God's Word, and you shall purpose to put any sin out of your life that your influence on others might be helpful and not a hindrance (Romans 14; 1 Timothy 3; Titus 1).

6. You are committed to unity, church teamwork, and biblical respect for church leadership (Philippians 2:1-4; Hebrews 13:7, 17).

7. You recognize, accept, pursue, and hold in highest regard the biblical instruction concerning family and marriage responsibility (Ephesians 5:22–6:4; Colossians 3:18-24; 1 Peter 3:1-7).

8. You are careful even in areas of Christian liberty or where the Bible is silent.

Name (Please Print)____

Date ____

Signature ____

First Methodist Church

"What Floats Your Boat" Sheet

Your team leader wants to get to know you! Give us some insight by completing this fun sheet, please.

Name:

1. What motivates you? (Write three or four lines on how you like to be encouraged.)

 ____

 ____

 ____

 ____

 ____

2. A daily encouragement for me would be:

 ____

 ____

3. If I could select a gift for myself for under $20, it would be:

 ____

 ____

4. If I had all day to do something for myself, I would:

 ____

 ____

5. The most fun I ever had was when:

6. My favorite hobby is:

7. My greatest passion in life is:

8. One area where I am growing is:

9. The greatest strength I possess is:

First Methodist Church

Children and Youth Ministry Volunteer Team Questionnaire

Legal Name (Last, First, Middle) ______________________________

Nickname ______________________________

Home phone ______________________________

Work phone ______________________________

Cell/pager ______________________________

Best time/place to call ______________________________

E-mail address ______________________________

Street address ______________________________

City/State/ZIP ______________________________

How long at your present address? ______________________________

If less than five years, give previous address and number of years:

Previous address ______________________________

Years there ______________________________

__Male __Female

Date of birth _____/_____/_____

Marital status ______________________________

If married, spouse's name ______________________________

Number of children ______________________________

Ages ______________________________

Emergency Contact

Name ______________________________

Relationship ______________________________

Phone number ______________________________

Occupation

Place of employment______________________________

Number of years______________________________

Employment history for last five years:

Employer's name/phone ______________________________

Employer's name/phone ______________________________

Employer's name/phone ______________________________

Do you have a personal relationship with Jesus Christ? Describe briefly.

____

____

____

How long have you attended First Methodist Church (FMC)?

____

List any leadership/volunteer experience you've had with children/youth:

____

____

____

List any training/education that has prepared you to work with children/youth:

____

____

____

List any other FMC ministries you're involved in:

____

____

Age/grade preference _______________________________

Hour preference _______________________________

Local Personal References

(must be 18 years old and not related to you)

Name _______________________________

Relationship _______________________________

Address _______________________________

Phone _______________________________

Comments (staff use)

____

____

Name _______________________________

Relationship _______________________________

Address _______________________________

Phone ______________________________

Comments (staff use)

____

____

Name ______________________________

Relationship ______________________________

Address______________________________

Phone ______________________________

Comments (staff use)

____

____

Applicant's Statement

I hereby authorize FMC to verify all information contained in this application with any references, my past or present employers, or any other appropriate personnel at my present or past employers, churches, or other organizations and any individuals to disclose any and all information to FMC. I release all such persons or entities from liability that may result or arise from FMC's collections of all such evaluations or information or its consideration of my application.

Should my application be accepted, I agree to follow the policies of FMC and to refrain from unscriptural conduct in the performance of my services on behalf of the church.

I understand that the personal information will be held confidential by the church staff.

Applicant's signature ______________________________

Date ______________________________

How to Establish a Volunteer Ministry Budget

What does it cost to create and maintain a volunteer equipping ministry? You may well be asked, and this handy worksheet will help you determine what your church can expect to spend. Keep in mind that even if you're using an office in the church and the church copier, there are costs associated with that overhead. Play fair—roll the appropriate prorated expenses into your budget.

And to keep things simple, figure annual costs. That's typically how church budgets are figured—though it's smart to check.

Personnel

Volunteer director ____________________

Administrative assistant

Additional staff ____________________

____________________ ____________________

____________________ ____________________

Benefits (estimate at ____% of total salaries) ____________________

Subtotal—Personnel $ ____________________

Overhead

Some of the items below are one-time purchases you'll need to make to set up an office. Others are line items you'll carry throughout the year.

Office furniture and equipment
Desks, chairs, lamps, etc.

File cabinets __________

Bulletin boards, white boards __________

Computer equipment __________

Audio-visual equipment __________

Additional equipment __________

Subtotal—Office furniture and equipment $ __________

Telephone

Land line __________

Mobile service __________

Subtotal—Telephone $ __________

Office supplies/expenses

Rent __________

Utilities __________

Office & maintenance supplies __________

Photocopying __________

Printing __________
(stationery, brochures, etc.)

Postage __________

Subtotal—Office supplies/expenses $ __________

Travel

Local
(mileage reimbursement, etc.) ________________

Long distance travel
(conferences, professional development) ________________

Subtotal—Travel $ ________________

Risk Management

Background checks ________________

Insurance ________________

Subtotal—Risk management $ ________________

Development and Training

Registration fees
(for conferences, seminars, etc.) ________________

Journal subscriptions, books, etc. ________________

Membership fees
(for professional associations) ________________

Handouts/books for training ________________

Refreshments ________________

Other training materials
(slides, films, etc.) ________________

Other ________________

Subtotal—Development and training $ ________________